LIGHT FROM THE DARKNESS
THE PAINTINGS OF PETER BIRKHÄUSER
COMMENTARY BY MARIE-LOUISE VON FRANZ

LICHT AUS DEM DUNKEL
DIE MALEREI VON PETER BIRKHÄUSER
KOMMENTARE VON MARIE-LOUISE VON FRANZ

LIGHT FROM THE DARKNESS
THE PAINTINGS OF PETER BIRKHÄUSER
COMMENTARY BY MARIE-LOUISE VON FRANZ

Edited by Kaspar Birkhäuser and Eva Wertenschlag-Birkhäuser

DAIMON
VERLAG

LICHT AUS DEM DUNKEL
DIE MALEREI VON PETER BIRKHÄUSER
KOMMENTARE VON MARIE-LOUISE VON FRANZ

Herausgegeben von Kaspar Birkhäuser und Eva Wertenschlag-Birkhäuser

DAIMON
VERLAG

STIFTUNG BIRKHÄUSER OERI

Front/Vorderseite: Peter Birkhäuser: Twin Fish/Zwillingsfisch
Back/Rückseite: Peter Birkhäuser: The Observer/Der Beobachter

ISBN 978-3-85630-798-1

www.daimon.ch
birkhaeuser-oeri.ch

"I was forced by the unconscious to fulfil a spiritual task, even if some of the products are not easy to understand."

– Peter Birkhäuser

Contents

Inhalt

1
MOTH
Watercolour and crayon, 1944/45

1
NACHTFALTER
Aquarell und Buntstift, 1944/45

Foreword to the new edition

This gem of a book *Licht aus dem Dunkel / Light from the Darkness* was first published in 1981, not long after the death of Peter Birkhäuser. It had originally been planned and designed by the artist himself. At the time, Marie-Louise von Franz had familiarized herself with the paintings he had selected and some of his dream diaries, and she formulated brief, illuminating commentaries, which reveal the archetypal dimensions of what can be seen. They might be described as poems.

The book, in both German and English, has always generated keen interest. It has now been expanded to include Marie-Louise von Franz's 1964 article: "Peter Birkhäuser – A Modern Artist who Strikes a New Path", translated by Michaela Kopp-Marx and made available for the first time in German. Michael Mitchell, the translator of the 1981 edition, has revised all the texts and provided an index. Some of the titles may vary from those used in the previous edition or in other books on Peter Birkhäuser's work; the painter tended to use different titles from time to time, as he pointed out himself in an interview in 1975. He said his understanding of them was continually evolving and that he did not intend the titles to be explanations of what they expressed.

Our thanks are due to the Research and Training Centre for Depth Psychology according to C. G. Jung and Marie-Louise von Franz for their generous financial support for the new edition.

Kaspar Birkhäuser and Eva Wertenschlag-Birkhäuser

Vorwort zur Neuausgabe

Kurz nach dem Tod von Peter Birkhäuser erschien 1981 dieses kostbare Buch *Licht aus dem Dunkel / Light from the Darkness*. Es war seinerzeit noch vom Künstler selbst geplant und gestaltet worden. Marie-Louise von Franz hat sich damals in die vom Verstorbenen ausgewählten Bilder und einige seiner Traumhefte vertieft und kurze, treffende Kommentare verfasst, die dem Betrachter die archetypischen Dimensionen öffnen. Es sind gleichsam Gedichte.

Das deutsch-englische Buch findet bis heute reges Interesse und wird hier neu publiziert. Es ist erweitert durch einen Artikel von Marie-Louise von Franz von 1964 «Peter Birkhäuser – A Modern Artist who Strikes a New Path», übersetzt von Michaela Kopp-Marx und hier erstmals auf Deutsch veröffentlicht. Michael Mitchell, dem 1981 die Übersetzungen gelangen, revidierte jetzt sämtliche Texte und fügte einen Index an. Die Titel der Gemälde variieren manchmal im Vergleich zur ersten Publikation und den weiteren Büchern zum Werk von Peter Birkhäuser. Der Maler selbst betitelte seine Bilder zuweilen anders, wie er selbst in einem Interview 1975 beschrieb. Er verstehe sie selber immer wieder neu und wolle mit seinen Titeln den Inhalt nicht erklären.

Wir danken der Stiftung des Forschungs- und Ausbildungszentrums für Tiefenpsychologie nach C. G. Jung und Marie-Louise von Franz für die grosszügige finanzielle Unterstützung der neuen Herausgabe.

Kaspar Birkhäuser und Eva Wertenschlag-Birkhäuser

THE PAINTER PETER BIRKHÄUSER

"Something was crossing me and destroying my conscious ideals, continuously, over a period of years, until I became so small that I had to give in. And I obeyed before I understood. From sheer suffering, I gave in. It was only later, over the years, that I was able to see the sense in it. But this unknown something within me had always known the sense [...]. I experienced a power within myself that was not me. That is religious experience. It forced me down a road which was not mine, nor was it a conscious choice; it did not correspond at all with my taste at that time. [...] It was a long road. But today, when I look back at the thousands of dreams and this whole process, the hard times and the sacrifices involved, I can see that it has been a very precious experience."

(Peter Birkhäuser in conversation with Dean L. Frantz, 1975)

Eva Wertenschlag-Birkhäuser, Kaspar Birkhäuser

Peter Birkhäuser was born on 7 June 1911 in Basel. His father was an ophthalmologist. Birkhäuser's childhood was overshadowed by the early death of his mother, but even as a child he had decided he wanted to be a painter. A medieval picture of a knight in armour in the Basel art gallery had fascinated him so much that he thought to himself: "I must become a painter. I want to learn to paint knights like that."

His urge to paint caused Birkhäuser to leave grammar school early and study at the college of art and design under the well-known Basel artist Niklaus Stoecklin. There followed two decades of professional activity which earned widespread recognition. With the artist's tools, Birkhäuser reproduced what he saw in nature and human beings using as much technical and aesthetic skill as he could apply. He tried to follow the example of the old masters, rejecting contemporary modern art because it seemed to him to be empty and have a merely destructive function.

He was extremely versatile in the production of paintings and drawings; he produced cartoons for the satirical magazine *Nebelspalter*, designed posters, ex libris plates, postage stamps, shop signs, labels, he sketched houses and landscapes on his travels, and he painted still-lifes, urban scenes, and, with increasing enthusiasm, portraits. His portraits had an unusually expressive quality, which, with his witty and unusual posters, made his work recognizable and sought-after. At the beginning of the nineteen-thirties he met his future wife Sibylle Oeri. They married in 1939.

One evening, while he was working in his studio, he saw a moth fluttering and settling on the outside of the window-pane. Birkhäuser turned this event into a painting (plate 1) in which the moth appears to be of monstrous proportions with an enormous wingspan. He interpreted this picture years later as a symbolic representation of his own state of mind at the time. The moth, an image of the soul, was prevented by the glass from reaching him in the light, in other words his consciousness. Indeed, Birkhäuser was completely cut off from the unconscious in those days. He had grown up in a somewhat rationalistic and agnostic parental environment, and his upbringing had led him to be hostile towards the spiritual or the religious.

The problems spontaneously indicated by the moth painting developed into a real crisis in Birkhäuser's life when he was about thirty. His artistic work refused to go smoothly. His attachment to tradition was a source of dissatisfaction to him. Constant and one-sided representations of external forms made him less and less happy. He lost his old enthusiasm for his work. Paintings required more and more effort. They stood around for long periods half-finished, and completing them only brought a sense of disgust. A crippling feeling of paralysis overcame him while painting, and he suffered more and more frequent bouts of depression.

It was in this state of perplexity that Birkhäuser and his wife came upon the ideas of C. G. Jung, and, impressed, began to note and analyse their dreams. Soon the dreams became recognizable as landmarks, unmistakably criticising Birkhäuser's tradition-bound style. One example among many similar ones was a dream in which Birkhäuser was at work on a painstakingly detailed study from nature when he noticed that in the middle of the act of drawing his hand was turning into a rigid horn.

The unconscious, however, was also drawing Birkhäuser's attention to new creative potentialities. Once this dream came to him: "I was in bed and had a woman beside me I didn't know. She told me to get up and go to the blue light. At first I was reluctant, too lazy. Then she ordered me again, and I did ..." The creative side of Birkhäuser's personality demanded a quest for a new spiritual value.

The artist and his wife both entered a Jungian analysis at this time. The analysis turned out to be for life. In the course of 35 years Birkhäuser collected and worked on more than 3400 of his own dreams.

One key dream from 1942 made it clear that from now on Birkhäuser should embark on his own individual path: in the dream the painter and his wife were being swept along in a vast stream of people all going the same way. All at once two giants in front of them turned to the left and strode off against the current of people pushing forwards. Birkhäuser and his wife followed them, but could hardly keep up with them for the tides of people continually dragging them the other way. The exertion of fighting their way through was finally rewarded when they came to a great table richly laden with good things.

Spiritual regeneration initiated a long period of questing in Birkhäuser's paintings. On the one hand he went on painting in his old style for many years, but at the same time, dissatisfied with that, he was attempting to placate the promptings of the unconscious with compromise solutions. During and towards the end of the forties he produced several paintings which could be called half realism and half fantasy. One of these shows immense flowers rising out of clouds and high above in the sky, at a great distance, a rowing-boat seen from below. In other words it still included objects which exist in the external world and had been studied minutely by the artist. The new factor was that these were now being combined in a more irrational composition.

So there was still a dissonance between what Birkhäuser was doing artistically and what his unconscious was telling him to do. A dream he had at the time illustrates this: On the way home Birkhäuser met a woman who led him into a vault with walls hung with copper baking moulds. He noticed particularly some big fish. Feeling pleased, he went on and came into a narrow passageway. In a dark corner stood an old woman threatening to kill him with a dagger. Fog began to swirl around him, thickening with every step he took nearer the woman, and in addition his eyes grew weaker. In terror he felt his way past her and successfully reached his front door. Now he could see clearly again, opened his letter box, and a vast amount of mail poured out.

In the dream the moulds represent Birkhäuser's opportunity to recast spiritual elements through art. The positive female figure – called in psychology the anima – shows him how to use this opportunity. But on the other hand he is threatened by a destructive side of himself which tries to chain him to a dead tradition and sterile art. Should he succeed in bypassing the witch and escaping her befogging effect on his consciousness, he will win through to his 'correspondence', i. e. to a treasure of inspiration. For Birkhäuser, overcoming dead tradition meant: "I had to give up all my old ideals one after another, which was very painful." Just how hard this struggle with himself must have been is suggested by the fact that it took the artist twelve years to make the great break and paint a picture entirely according to his own imagination, with no model from the external world.

In 1953 Birkhäuser painted "The World's Wound" (plate 2). "In rage and despair I smudged the picture on to the canvas with no faith that anything reasonable would come out." The painter often stressed that this picture of a split man was in no sense a product of his conscious will. He had simply bowed to necessity after four years of being haunted by that face in his dreams.

This picture was Birkhäuser's breakthrough to what could be called paintings of the imagination. In other words he began to put forms and images from the unconscious on canvas without any kind of model from external reality and free from slavish conscious control.

The painter himself said about his imaginative pictures: "I can't always bring it out at the first attempt, because it's difficult to keep in touch with the intuition that is guiding me. Then sometimes I find the right form of expression at once, or to put it more accurately: it reveals itself suddenly. Mostly it is like groping in the dark, fetching it out. From time to time I find myself on the wrong track without noticing it. Then a very critical dream may emerge, and I realize that I shall have to start all over again. It can drive one to despair. Then I try again and to my surprise the painting assumes a totally unexpected form. Usually the unconscious presents me with a new content, an attractive form or an idea, or sometimes it seems to ambush me. But then I have to find a way of putting it on canvas. To have the right attitude is a very serious problem; I'm glad I had the opportunity of discussing this with Jung."

Jung said: "The dream provides the impulse, but it is only a sketch, a cartoon, you have to develop it and give it form."

To which Birkhäuser replied: "But I'm always afraid I will distort the original notion too much. In transferring such a delicate insubstantial thing to canvas with thick oil colours it often tends to change. Additional ideas which were not in the original impulse begin to obtrude."

Jung answered: "That doesn't matter, that too is part of the unconscious impulse."

The process cited here took time to bring about. Birkhäuser had to make a fresh effort for each new picture. Looking at the paintings of his final 25 years it becomes clear how he increasingly succeeded in fulfilling the promptings of the unconscious. His images resemble less and less the shapes of the external world, and lose their material quality.

One of the techniques which produce this effect is that light and shade disappear and the painted forms seem to be light themselves.

But the thing which is of most general interest in the paintings from the imagination is that they reflect not only the artist's own personal psychological situation but that they reveal images from the collective unconscious which concern our whole age and culture. Paintings like "The World's Wound" (plate 2), "Imprisoned Creative Power" (plate 8), "The Outcast" (plate 10), or "God's Fire" (plate 25) have something to say to us all.

From the moment Birkhäuser introduced the first of these dream images to the public, he was met with blank incomprehension. As his paintings introduced genuinely new subject matter, the art world rejected them. Many of Birkhäuser's own friends were alienated, so that the painter became increasingly isolated. During this time he was unable to support himself from his painting and was forced to live from advertising work. Only gradually did a new group of people appear who appreciated and bought his paintings; many of them were younger people, often from America. In this period of obscurity and lack of public success three personal relationships stood him in particularly good stead. His wife was unshakably loyal and a constructive critic. He also enjoyed decisive support from his analyst and friend Marie-Louise von Franz. In addition, another painter and his closest friend, Erhard Jacoby, was making similar attempts to represent images from the unconscious.

In 1969 he lost his friend Jacoby, and in 1971 his wife. That year saw the beginning of a serious lung complaint, but increasing physical handicaps in the last five years of his life were accompanied by striking progress in his spiritual development and artistic productivity. He devoted himself exclusively to painting and the task set by images from the unconscious.

Having kept a full and detailed diary of his dreams, Birkhäuser was able to look back over 35 years of his life. Now he could discern a sense of purpose in the way the unconscious had steered him along a path he had been reluctant to follow. This prompted Birkhäuser's comment, not the product of any theory, but of personal experience: "This mysterious power has its own will and intention. It knows things that no human being can know. So I'm sure it would not be wrong to give it the name of God. It is after all greater than every human faculty. It is what we impute to God, to know the future, or to know what an individual is to do in the decades ahead." *(Peter Birkhäuser in conversation with Dean L. Frantz, 1975)*

N.B. Quotations are adapted from interviews with Birkhäuser conducted by Dean L. Frantz while he was working on a diploma thesis "Meaning for Modern Man in the Paintings of Peter Birkhäuser", Jung Institute, Zürich 1977 (unpublished).

DER MALER PETER BIRKHÄUSER

«Etwas durchkreuzte mich und zerstörte meine bewussten Ideale, konsequent über Jahre, bis ich so klein war, dass ich nachgab. Und ich gehorchte, noch bevor ich es begriff. [...] Erst später, mit den Jahren, konnte ich endlich den Sinn erkennen. Aber dieses Unbekannte in mir wusste den Sinn schon immer. [...] Ich erlebte eine Macht in mir, die nicht ich war. Das ist religiöse Erfahrung. Sie zwang mich auf einen Weg, der nicht von mir gewollt war, der nicht meinem damaligen Geschmack entsprach. [...] Es war ein langer Weg. Aber heute, wenn ich zurückschaue auf die Tausenden von Träumen und diese lange Entwicklung und die Opfer, sehe ich, dass es eine sehr kostbare Erfahrung war.» (Peter Birkhäuser im Gespräch mit Dean L. Frantz, 1975)

Eva Wertenschlag-Birkhäuser, Kaspar Birkhäuser

Peter Birkhäuser wurde am 7. Juni 1911 in Basel geboren. Sein Vater war Augenarzt. Birkhäusers Kindheit wurde durch den frühen Tod der Mutter überschattet. Schon als Kind stand für ihn fest, dass er später Maler werden wollte. Im Kunstmuseum Basel begeisterte ihn nämlich die mittelalterliche Darstellung eines Ritters derartig, dass er dachte: «Ich muss Maler werden. Ich will lernen, solche Ritter zu malen.»

Sein Drang zum Malen veranlasste Birkhäuser, das Gymnasium vorzeitig zu verlassen und sich an der Kunstgewerbeschule und bei dem bekannten Basler Maler Niklaus Stoecklin auszubilden. Es folgte in den nächsten zwei Jahrzehnten eine berufliche Tätigkeit, die allseits Anerkennung fand. Birkhäuser stellte mit Pinsel und Stift möglichst schön, ästhetisch und technisch perfekt dar, was er in der Natur und bei den Menschen sah. Seine Vorbilder waren die alten Meister. Die moderne Kunst seiner Zeit lehnte er ab, weil sie ihm leer und als blosse Destruktion des traditionellen Weltbilds vorkam.

Als Kunstmaler und Graphiker betätigte er sich äusserst vielseitig. Er zeichnete für die satirische Zeitschrift *Nebelspalter*, malte Plakate, entwarf Exlibris, Briefmarken, Fassadenschriften, Etiketten, zeichnete auf Reisen Häuser und Landschaften, malte Stillleben, Blumen, Stadtszenerien und mit zunehmender Liebe Porträts. Seine Porträts hatten durch ihre Beseeltheit eine besondere Qualität und machten ihn ebenso wie seine originellen Plakate beliebt und bekannt. Zu Beginn der dreissiger Jahre lernte er seine Lebensgefährtin, Sibylle Oeri, kennen, die er 1939 heiratete.

Als er eines Abends in seinem Atelier arbeitete, setzte sich von aussen ein Nachtfalter an die Fensterscheibe. Den Anblick dieses Tiers setzte Birkhäuser in ein Gemälde um, das den Falter in unheimlicher Grösse mit meterbreiter Flügelspannweite zeigt (Abb. 1). Im Alter interpretierte er dieses Bild als eine symbolische Darstellung seines damaligen geistigen Zustandes: Der Falter als Bild für das Seelische wurde durch die Fensterscheibe daran gehindert, zu ihm ans Licht, das heisst in sein Bewusstsein, zu kommen.

Und tatsächlich war Birkhäuser damals gänzlich abgespalten vom Unbewussten. Aufgewachsen in einem eher aufklärerisch-rationalistischen Elternhaus, hatte er eine deutlich negative Einstellung dem Seelischen und Religiösen gegenüber.

Die im Falterbild ungewollt dargestellte Problematik entwickelte sich für Birkhäuser, als er etwa dreissig Jahre alt war, zu einer eigentlichen Lebenskrise. Bei seiner künstlerischen Arbeit tauchten Schwierigkeiten auf. Seine Befangenheit in der Tradition wurde für ihn unbefriedigend. Die ständige einseitige Darstellung von Äusserem machte den Maler mehr und mehr unglücklich. Er verlor die alte Begeisterung an seinem Schaffen. Bilder kamen nur noch mit Mühe zustande. Lange standen sie unfertig umher. Und nur mit Gefühlen der Unlust vollendete Birkhäuser sie schliesslich. Er fühlte sich oft wie gelähmt beim Malen. Immer häufiger verfiel er in Depressionen.

In ihrer damaligen Ratlosigkeit stiessen Birkhäuser und seine Frau auf die Gedankenwelt C. G. Jungs, und beeindruckt davon begannen sie, ihre Träume zu beobachten und zu analysieren. Und die Träume erwiesen sich bald als konkrete Orientierungshilfen. Unmissverständlich kritisierten sie etwa Birkhäusers traditionelle Malerei. Ein Beispiel von vielen ähnlichen ist das folgende: Im Traum war Birkhäuser mit einer sorgfältigen Naturstudie beschäftigt, als er mit Schrecken feststellte, wie seine zeichnende Hand zu unbewegbarem Horn erstarrte.

Vom Unbewussten her wurde Birkhäuser aber auch auf neue Möglichkeiten seiner schöpferischen Tätigkeit aufmerksam gemacht. Damals träumte es ihm: «Ich lag im Bett und hatte eine unbekannte Frau neben mir. Sie hiess mich aufzustehen und zum blauen Licht zu gehen. Erst wollte ich nicht, aus Bequemlichkeit. Da befahl sie es mir nochmals, worauf ich ging ...» – Birkhäusers schöpferische Seite verlangte von ihm eine Suchwanderung nach einem neuen geistigen Wert.

Der Künstler und seine Frau begannen in jenen Jahren beide eine Jungsche Analyse. Es sollten Lebensanalysen werden, die bis zu beider Tod dauerten. Birkhäuser sammelte und verarbeitete während 35 Jahren über 3400 eigene Träume.

Ein Schlüsseltraum von 1942 machte deutlich, dass Birkhäuser fortan einen ganz eigenen Weg einzuschlagen hatte: Der Maler liess sich im Traum mit seiner Frau in einem gigantischen Menschenstrom in eine gewisse Richtung treiben. Plötzlich wichen vor ihnen zwei Riesen nach links ab und schritten quer gegen den Menschenstrom voran. Birkhäuser und seine Frau schlossen sich ihnen an, konnten ihnen aber kaum folgen, weil sie von den ihnen entgegenströmenden Menschen immer wieder weggerissen wurden. Nach langem, äusserst anstrengendem Vorwärtskämpfen erreichten sie eine grosse, reichgedeckte Tafel. An dieser wurden sie zum Lohn für ihre Mühen reich bewirtet.

Sein geistiger Neubeginn löste in Birkhäusers malerischem Schaffen eine lange Periode des Suchens aus. Einesteils malte er noch viele Jahre in seinem alten Stil weiter und, unbefriedigt davon, versuchte er andernteils, die Stimme des Unbewussten mit Kompromissmalerei zu beruhigen. In der Mitte und gegen das Ende der vierziger Jahre schuf er einige Bilder, die man halb realistisch, halb phantastisch nennen könnte. Eines jener Bilder etwa zeigt riesige, aus Wolken aufsteigende Blumen und hoch oben am Himmel, in grosser Entfernung, ein von unten gesehenes Ruderboot. Es waren darauf also weiterhin Dinge zu sehen, die in der äusseren Welt existierten und vom Maler genau beobachtet und studiert worden waren. Neu war nur, dass sie zu einer Art von irrationaler Komposition verwertet worden waren.

Es blieb folglich weiterhin ein Zwiespalt bestehen zwischen Birkhäusers künstlerischem Schaffen und dem, was das Unbewusste von ihm verlangte. Ein damaliger Traum weist auf diesen Zwiespalt hin: Auf dem Weg nach Hause begegnete Birkhäuser einer Frau, die ihn in ein Kellergewölbe führte, dessen Wände reich mit kupfernen Backformen behängt waren. Grosse Fische fielen ihm darunter auf. Beglückt setzte er seinen Weg fort und gelangte in eine enge Gasse. Dort stand in einer dunklen Mauerecke eine Alte mit einem Dolch, die nach seinem Leben trachtete. Nebel begann sich zu bilden und wurde rasch dichter, je näher Birkhäuser, der zusätzlich von einer Augenschwäche befallen wurde, der Alten kam. Angstvoll tastete er sich an ihr vorbei und erreichte glücklich seine Haustür. Er sah jetzt wieder klar, öffnete seinen Briefkasten, und eine Unmenge von Post quoll ihm entgegen.

In diesem Traum verbildlichen die Kupferformen Birkhäusers Möglichkeit, seelische Inhalte künstlerisch neu zu fassen. Die positive Frauengestalt – in psychologischer Sprache seine Anima – öffnet ihm den Zugang zu dieser Möglichkeit. Andererseits ist die Bedrohung durch eine destruktive Seite in ihm, die ihn an tote Tradition und Materie binden will, dargestellt. Gelingt es Birkhäuser, der Hexe aus dem Weg zu gehen und ihrer das Bewusstsein benebelnden Wirkung nicht zu verfallen, erhält er Zugang zu seiner Post, das heisst zu reichen Inspirationen.

Tote Tradition zu überwinden, bedeutete für Birkhäuser: «Ich musste unter grossen Schmerzen Stück für Stück alle meine alten Ideale aufgeben.» Wie zäh und hart der Kampf und Konflikt mit sich selbst gewesen sein mussten, zeigt allein der Umstand, dass es zwölf Jahre dauerte, bis es dem Künstler gelang, den wesentlichen Schritt zu tun und ohne jedes Vorbild aus der äussern Welt ein Bild rein einer inneren Vorstellung folgend zu malen.

1953 schuf Birkhäuser das Gemälde «Der Gespaltene» (Abb. 2). «Ich schmierte das Bild voller Wut und Verzweiflung auf die Leinwand, ohne Glaube, dass etwas Rechtes dabei herauskommen werde.» Der Maler betonte übrigens, dass die Abbildung des Gespaltenen keineswegs durch seinen Willen zustande gekommen sei. Vielmehr sei er dem reinen Zwang gewichen. Vier Jahre habe ihn das Traumbild dieses Gespaltenen nämlich verfolgt.

Mit dem «Gespaltenen» war Birkhäuser der Durchbruch zur sogenannten Phantasiemalerei gelungen. Er begann also, unter Verzicht auf Vorbilder aus der äusseren Realität und auf jegliche Lenkung durch das Bewusstsein, Formen und Inhalte aus dem Unbewussten auf die Leinwand zu bannen. Der Maler äusserte sich zur Entstehungsweise seiner Phantasiebilder folgendermassen:

«Oft gelingt es mir nicht, ein Bild beim ersten Versuch hervorzubringen, weil es schwierig ist, den Kontakt zur führenden Intuition aufrechtzuerhalten. Dann wieder finde ich den passenden Ausdruck auf Anhieb – oder besser: er enthüllt sich mir plötzlich. Meist ist es wie ein Tasten im Dunkeln, ein Hervorsuchen. Manchmal gerate ich auf eine falsche Spur, ohne es zu merken. Dann mag ein Traum mit scharfer Kritik auftauchen. Und ich weiss, dass ich von vorne beginnen muss. Verzweifelt und unsicher suche ich nach einem neuen Weg, und zu meiner Überraschung nimmt das Gemälde plötzlich Formen an, über die ich zuvor nichts gewusst habe. – Meist bringt mir das Unbewusste einen neuen Inhalt nahe, eine Gestalt oder eine Idee, ja oft überfällt es mich damit. Dann aber muss ich einen

Weg finden, es auf die Leinwand zu bringen. Dazu die richtige Einstellung zu finden, ist ein ernstes Problem. Ich bin froh, dass ich darüber mit Jung sprechen konnte.»

Jung habe ihm gesagt: «Der Traum gibt den Anstoss, ist aber erst eine Ahnung. Und Sie müssen sie ans Licht ziehen und ihr Gestalt geben.»

Worauf Birkhäuser erwidert habe: «Ich befürchte beim Malen aber immer, diese Ahnung zu sehr zu verformen. Indem ich eine solch zarte, unstoffliche Sache mit dicker Ölfarbe auf die Leinwand übertrage, neigt sie oft dazu, verändert zu werden. Zusätzliche Ideen, die ursprünglich nicht in diesem Anstoss enthalten waren, beginnen einzufliessen.»

Jung dazu: «Das macht nichts, auch das gehört zum Impuls aus dem Unbewussten.»

Was in diesem Zitat geschildert worden ist, konnte Birkhäuser aber nur langsam verwirklichen. Er musste sich beim Malen jeden Bildes neu darum bemühen. Wenn man auf die Bilder seiner letzten 25 Schaffensjahre blickt, erkennt man, wie es ihm zunehmend gelungen ist, den Anstössen aus dem Unbewussten zu entsprechen. Das Dargestellte erinnert immer weniger an Formen aus der äusseren Welt und verliert alle Stofflichkeit. Zu dieser neuen Qualität trägt unter anderem Folgendes bei: Es gibt nicht mehr Licht und Schatten, sondern die gemalten Gestalten scheinen selbst Licht zu sein.

Was aber Birkhäusers Phantasiemalerei in das allgemeine Interesse rückt, ist, dass durch sie nicht nur die persönliche seelische Situation des Künstlers gespiegelt wird, sondern dass sie Bilder aus dem kollektiven Unbewussten sichtbar macht, dass sie unser aller Kultur und Zeit betrifft. Bilder wie «Der Gespaltene» (Abb. 2), «Tier im Berg» (Abb. 8), «Der Ausgestossene» (Abb. 10) oder «Gottes Feuer» (Abb. 25) gehen uns alle an.

Sobald Birkhäuser mit seinen ersten Traumbildern an die Öffentlichkeit trat, stiess er auf gänzliches Unverständnis. Da seine Gemälde wirklich neue Inhalte zeigen, lehnte die Welt der Kunst sie ab. Viele Freunde Birkhäusers waren befremdet, so dass der Maler mehr und mehr isoliert wurde. Während Jahren konnte er seinen Lebensunterhalt nicht mehr aus der Malerei bestreiten und war ganz auf Werbegraphik angewiesen. Nur langsam bildete sich ein neuer Kreis von Interessierten, die seine Phantasiebilder verstanden und kauften. Es waren vorwiegend Amerikaner und jüngere Leute. In jener Zeit, in der Birkhäuser mit seiner Kunst in der Öffentlichkeit einen so schweren Stand hatte, halfen ihm drei menschliche Beziehungen in besonderer Weise. Seine Frau hielt ihm unerschütterlich die Treue und war ihm eine konstruktive Kritikerin. Weiteren entscheidenden Rückhalt bot ihm seine Analytikerin und Freundin Marie-Louise von Franz. Erhard Jacoby, sein engster Freund und selber auch Maler, bemühte sich wie er, Inhalte aus dem Unbewussten darzustellen.

1969 verlor er seinen Freund Jacoby, 1971 seine Gattin. Seit damals litt Birkhäuser zunehmend unter einer schweren Lungenkrankheit. Seine letzten fünf Lebensjahre wurden für ihn aber zu einer Zeit besonderer seelischer Entwicklung und künstlerischer Fruchtbarkeit. Er widmete sich ausschliesslich seiner Malerei und der Auseinandersetzung mit dem Unbewussten. Anhand seiner umfangreichen Traumaufzeichnungen blickte Birkhäuser auf seine letzten 35 Lebensjahre zurück. In der Art, wie ihn das Unbewusste in eine von ihm ungewollte Richtung gelenkt hatte, konnte er jetzt Sinn und Folgerichtigkeit feststellen. Daher sagte Peter Birkhäuser nicht aufgrund theoretischer Überlegung, sondern aus eigener Erfahrung: «Diese unbekannte Kraft hat ihren eigenen Willen und ihre eigene Absicht. Sie weiss Dinge, die kein Mensch wissen kann. Daher ist es gewiss nicht falsch, wenn man sie Gott nennt. Ihr Wissen steht ja über allen menschlichen Möglichkeiten. Nur eine gottähnliche Kraft kann die Zukunft kennen und wissen, was für mich zu tun in den nächsten Jahrzehnten das Richtige ist.» *(Peter Birkhäuser im Gespräch mit Dean L. Frantz, 1975)*

Die Zitate entstammen einem englischsprachigen Interview mit Birkhäuser für die Arbeit «Meaning for Modern Man in the Paintings of Peter Birkhäuser», Diplomarbeit von Dean L. Frantz am Jung-Institut, Zürich 1977, unpubliziert.

PLATES
COMMENTARIES

Peter Birkhäuser's pictures are pure products of the unconscious. These commentaries do not represent any conscious thoughts of the artist's. They are attempts subsequently to achieve some understanding of the paintings and thus to hint at possible interpretations.

Marie-Louise von Franz

BILDER
KOMMENTARE

Peter Birkhäuser hat seine Bilder rein aus dem Unbewussten heraus geschaffen. Diese Kommentare entsprechen keinen bewussten Gedanken des Malers. Sie sind Versuche, nachträglich etwas von dieser Malerei zu verstehen und die Bilder so dem Betrachter andeutungsweise zu erschliessen.

Marie-Louise von Franz

2
THE WORLD'S WOUND

In a dream this man was desperately trying to reach P. B. He embodies the tragic inner split of the modern individual, who, through reliance on rationality, has lost the spirituality of natural man. We can no longer overcome this split, but we can become conscious of it. Then the creative spirit of the unconscious could be reintegrated with our consciousness. The eye on the left is opened in fearful vision; that on the right remains sceptical and cool. It was after this encounter that P. B. felt urged to give up painting motifs of his own choice and devote himself to representing the sufferings of our age as reflected in the unconscious.
Oil, January 1953

2
DER GESPALTENE

In einem Traum versuchte dieser Mann verzweifelt, P. B. zu erreichen. Er verkörpert die Tragik des modernen Menschen, der durch seine rationale Welteinstellung die Weltsicht des natürlichen Menschen verdrängt hat. Wir können diese Spaltung nicht mehr aufheben, aber ihrer bewusst werden, so dass sich dann der Geist des Unbewussten schöpferisch mit dem Bewusstsein verbinden könnte. Das linke Auge ist angstvoll sehend aufgerissen, das rechte blickt sachlich-skeptisch. Von dieser Begegnung an fühlte sich P. B. gedrängt, nicht mehr Motive seiner eigenen Wahl, sondern des Leidens unserer Zeit, wie es sich im Unbewussten spiegelt, zu malen.
Öl, Januar 1953

3

THE CAT

The 'old woman' with her predator's claws and her mysterious animal gaze. In dreams she threatened the artist's life, but also appeared as the guardian of undiscovered spiritual treasures. She is the 'Great Mother' who can paralyse those who long to regress to her, but who also possesses the age-old wisdom of nature. In later dreams she also appeared as a murderous praying mantis. Her dark side mirrors a negative conscious attitude towards her, which gives her that lurking yet expectant look, as if acceptance of her could reveal a completely different side. Then she could become, like the Egyptian cat goddess Bastet, a bringer of joy and vitality.
Oil, between 1949 and 1955

3

DIE KATZE

Die «Alte» mit ihren Raubtierklauen und ihrem geheimnisvollen Tierblick. Sie trachtet dem Maler nach dem Leben und ist zugleich die Hüterin noch zu entdeckender seelischer Schätze. Sie ist die «Grosse Mutter», zu der sich zurückzusehnen lähmt und die doch das uralte Wissen der Natur besitzt. Später erschien sie in Träumen auch als mörderische Gottesanbeterin. Ihre finstere Seite ist eine Spiegelung einer negativen Bewusstseinseinstellung zu ihr, daher ihr lauernder, erwartungsvoller Blick, als ob sie, wenn sie angenommen würde, eine ganz andere Seite enthüllen könnte; dann würde sie wie die ägyptische Katzengöttin Bastet eine Spenderin der Lebensfreude.
Öl, zwischen 1949 und 1955

4
DEPRESSION

Every new creation is preceded by an annihilation of the prior world of consciousness. Everything has become stale and meaningless, and the unknown creature from the depths of the psyche reaches out to suck at the painter with tentacles like mist, like liquid or ectoplasm. Depression dissolves his head, as he sits unproductively with his back to the easel, suspended in space, with nothing solid beneath his feet. Only by turning round to face the uncanny powers can he discover their secret intentions.
Oil, 1954/55

4
DEPRESSION

Jeder neuen Schöpfung geht eine Vernichtung der bisherigen Bewusstseinswelt voraus; alles ist schal und sinnlos geworden. Die Depression löst dem Maler, der untätig dasitzt, den Kopf auf. Sie ist wie untastbare Nebelschleier. Mit tausend Tentakeln ausgerüstet, saugt sich das Unbekannte der Seelentiefe an ihn an – wie Wasser oder wie Nebel oder Ektoplasma.
Erst wenn wir uns umkehren und diesem Unheimlichen ins Gesicht blicken, offenbart es seine geheimen Absichten. Der Maler sitzt im leeren Raum – er hat keinen Boden mehr unter den Füssen.
Öl, 1954/55

5
COMING UP

The "ugliest man" (Nietzsche) comes up from the depths of the sewers, hunchbacked, scrawny and wretched. His expression mirrors the sadness of someone who has never been loved, for we have turned away from our unconscious soul. But in folklore a hunchback is a bringer of luck; he carries a lamp, a chance to bring light into the darkness of our disordered world.
Oil, ca. 1954/55

5
DER AUFSTEIGENDE

Bucklig, schmächtig und elend steigt der «hässliche Mensch» (Nietzsche) aus der Tiefe der Kanalisation. Sein Ausdruck spiegelt das Elend eines Menschen wider, der nie Liebe erfuhr, weil wir uns von unserer Seele abgewandt haben. Aber ein Buckliger bringt nach dem Volksglauben Glück – er trägt ein Licht, die Möglichkeit, die Dunkelheit unserer verfahrenen Welt zu erhellen.
Öl, etwa 1954/55

6
THE INWARD GAZE

If we look inwards, the 'other side' looks at us too. The unconscious begins to unveil its secret play of fantasy: images of seductive beauty and the cruellest abysses of nature. They are framed above by a transparent snake, a symbol of the spirit. Often P. B. was persecuted in his dreams by a strange 'old woman', an unrecognisable, terrifying creature. This represents the dark side of nature, inertia and death, from which the creative artist has to wrestle free again and again. The figure who sees this vision is colourless – his consciousness is drained of life, and the whole play of colours has gone into the reality of his unconscious, where a frog rises from below, a symbol of resurrection and rebirth.
Oil, 1954/55

6
DER EINWÄRTSBLICKENDE

Wenn wir nach innen schauen, blickt die «andere Seite» auch zu uns herüber. Das Unbewusste beginnt, sein Phantasiespiel zu enthüllen: Bilder von verlockender Schönheit und die grausamsten Abgründe der Natur. – Oben ist eine durchsichtige Schlange, ein Symbol des Geistes. Oft war P. B. in Träumen von einer «Alten», einem unerkennbaren, furchtbaren Wesen, verfolgt. Es stellt die dunkle Seite der Natur dar, Inertie und Tod, aus der sich der schöpferische Mensch immer wieder herausreissen muss. Der nach innen Schauende ist farblos – kein Leben ist mehr in ihm, und das ganze Farbenspiel hat sich in die Wirklichkeit der Seele verlegt, wo unten ein Frosch, ein Symbol der Auferstehung und Wiedergeburt, aufsteigt.
Öl, 1954/55

7
THE FOURTH DIMENSION

This picture is based on a vision which came to P. B. on 14 September 1956 and was painted in 1956/57. C. G. Jung was enthusiastic about it and comments on it in detail in his paper "Flying Saucers: A Modern Myth" (C. G. Jung: Collected Works, vol. 10, § 736 ff.). The town portrays our usual conscious three-dimensional world, and through it flows the world of an incommensurable fourth dimension, right down into the solid earth but without touching the town. It is a sort of cosmic background, also a 'source of living waters'. In it appear vague faces and eyes, some clear, some dim, partly animal and partly human. The vision portrays the 'other side' of our world, the unconscious, in which a new God-image becomes dimly visible.
Oil, 1956/57

7
DIE VIERTE DIMENSION

Aufgrund einer Vision vom 14. September 1956 gemalt. Die Stadt stellt wohl unsere gewöhnliche dreidimensionale Welt dar. Eine vierte, mit ihr inkommensurable Dimension durchströmt sie – sogar bis in die Tiefen der soliden Erde. Sie bildet einen Welthintergrund, der auch ein «Quell lebendigen Wassers» ist. In ihm erscheinen Augen und drei angedeutete Gesichter, von einem vierten dominiert. Sie sind teils tierisch, teils menschlich. Es ist dies die «andere Seite» unserer Welt, das Unbewusste, in welchem sich ein Gottesbild andeutet. C. G. Jung war von diesem Bild begeistert und bespricht es ausführlich in: «Ein neuer Mythus» (GW 10, § 736 ff.).
Öl, 1956/57

8
IMPRISONED CREATIVE POWER

The "Archaeus" of Paracelsus, the underground fiery creative power of nature which could erupt and destroy our world. Flames shoot out of the mountain and stones thunder down. At the bottom on the right a man leaves his tiny car and runs away in terror. But the round golden eye of the animal is like a seed of light in the darkness, suggesting insight and growing consciousness. Like the eye of a bird, it focuses on what is distant rather than nearby. The animal is a sort of Behemoth, the dark female side of God, waiting to be liberated from its prison in the depths of the earth.
Oil, 1958

8
TIER IM BERG

Der paracelsische «Archaeus», der feurige Schöpfergeist der Natur im Bergesinneren, eine Urmacht, die ausbrechend unsere Welt vernichten könnte. Flammen schlagen aus dem Berg, und Steine rollen krachend herab. Rechts unten ein kleines Auto und ein flüchtender Mensch. Aber das runde, goldene Auge des Tiers wirkt wie ein Lichtkeim in der Finsternis, Einsicht und Bewusstwerdung andeutend. Es ist wie ein Vogelauge – es blickt in die Ferne, nicht auf Naheliegendes. Das Tier ist wohl eine Art von Behemoth, die weibliche, dunkle Seite der Gottheit, welche auf Befreiung aus der Tiefe wartet.
Öl, 1958

9
FIRE GIVES BIRTH

The sea of flames of the Godhead, giving birth to all the colourful and wondrous forms and shapes of nature, out of which the human being, too, emerges into the suffering and beauty of life.
Oil, 1959/60

9
FEUERGEBURT

Das Flammenmeer der Gottheit, das alle bunten, wundersamen Gestalten und Formen der Natur gebiert, aus dem auch der Mensch in das Leiden und die Schönheit des Lebens hineingeboren wird.
Öl, 1959/60

10
THE OUTCAST

From the grey monotony of the industrial city with its functional technology the spirit of the soul, the creative secret of nature, is banished. With heavy steps he retreats towards the left, into the unconscious. He trails behind him a tail of flames, which is also a rainbow. The latter hints that reconciliation with God is still possible, but the fire could also destroy all our towns. The face of this outcast spirit is split in two, like the man with "The World's Wound" (plate 2); one half is green, the colour of nature, and one blue or spiritual – the *Mercurius duplex* of the alchemists, good for the good and evil for the evil.
Oil, 1960

10
DER AUSGESTOSSENE

In der grauen Eintönigkeit der Industriestadt und der reinen Zweckmässigkeit ihrer Technik ist der Geist der Seele, das schöpferische Geheimnis des Naturgeistes, verbannt. Mit schweren Schritten zieht er sich nach links, ins Unbewusste, zurück, einen Flammenschweif, der zugleich Regenbogen ist, nach sich ziehend. Versöhnung mit dem Gott ist noch möglich, wie der Regenbogen beweist. Aber dieser Geist kann auch unsere Städte in einem Flammenmeer vernichten. Sein Antlitz ist zweigeteilt wie das des «Gespaltenen» (Abb. 2), in eine grüne, naturhafte und eine blaue, geistige Hälfte. Er ist der *Mercurius duplex* der Alchemisten, gut mit den Guten und böse mit den Bösen.
Öl, 1960

11
PUER AETERNUS

The new spirit of the coming age of Aquarius, riding on a white beast (Pegasus) half horse, half boar. Wherever he stretches his hands, new life begins to bloom. This is the child predicted in Revelation as the boy who was snatched up to heaven and is, according to Jung, an image of totality in man.

Eternal youth, with unending agelessness, you
Stand in your bloom at the height of the heavens,
Seen, your head without horns, like a virgin,
The east in your thrall out to black India
Where the Ganges meets the furthest border.
(Ovid, Metamorphoses, 4,18, trans. MM)

Oil, April 1960

11
PUER AETERNUS

Der neue Geist des kommenden Aquariuszeitalters, auf einem weissen Eberpferd (Pegasus) reitend. Wohin er seine Hände streckt, erblühen neue Formen. Er wurde vorausgesagt in der Offenbarung Johannis als jener Knabe, der in den Himmel entrückt wurde, und ist, wie Jung es auslegte, ein Bild des «vollständigen Menschen».

Unvergänglich ist blühender Jüngling deine Jugend,
Und du wirst der Schönste gesehen
In dem hohen Olymp.
Ohne Hörner erscheinst du
Wie ein Mädchen gestaltet …
(Ovid, Metamorphosen, 4,18)

Öl, April 1960

12
TWIN FISH

The future world saviour in his double form still hidden in the fish in the depths of the ocean. The fish's eye is like a flower – earth's answer to the light of the sun. The huge blue eye at the top left suggests that something in the cosmic background sees everything. Within the fish mortal and immortal man hold each other in a close embrace.

Two birds, inseparable winged friends,
Cling to one and the same tree.
One of them eats the sweet fruit;
The other looks on, but does not eat.
In such a tree the miserable spirit,
Bewildered, grieves its impotence,
But seeing the other – the god's – fulfilment
And majesty, his grief will pass.
(Shvetâshvatara Uphanishad, IV,6.)
Oil, 1961

12
ZWILLINGSFISCH

Die Doppelgestalt des kommenden Weltenheilands, noch im Fisch verborgen in der Tiefe des Weltmeeres. Das Auge des Fisches ist wie eine Blume, eine Antwort der Erde auf das Sonnenlicht. Ein blaues Riesenauge im Hintergrund deutet an, dass etwas im Welthintergrund alles sieht. Die zwei Gestalten im Fischinnern sind der sterbliche und der unsterbliche Mensch.

Zwei schön beflügelte, verbundene Freunde
Umarmen einen und denselben Baum.
Einer von ihnen speist die süsse Beere,
Der andre schaut, nicht essend, nur herab.
Zu solchem Baum der Geist, herabgesunken,
In seiner Ohnmacht grämt sich wahnbefangen,
Doch wenn er ehrt und schaut des andern Allmacht
Und Majestät, dann weicht von ihm sein Kummer.
(Shvetâshvatara-Uphanishad, IV,6.)
Öl, 1961

13

A BIRTH

Out of what looks like a mass of intestines or brainfolds, i. e. out of areas of the psyche far removed from consciousness, a human spirit being is born, not on to the earth, but into free space. This being is simultaneously an eight-petalled flower, which has always symbolised psychic totality, like the ‘golden flower’ of the alchemists and Taoists. It is the image of the resurrection of the inner man, the self.
Oil, 1961

13

GEBURT AUS DEM JENSEITS

Aus einer Masse, die wie Gedärme oder Hirnwindungen aussieht – völlig bewusstseinsferne Bereiche der Seele andeutend –, wird nach rechts (in Richtung des Bewusstseins) ein menschliches Geistwesen geboren. Es ist der «ewige Mensch», der auch wie eine achtblättrige Blume erscheint, ein Bild des Seelenzentrums. Die Alchemisten nannten ihre vier- oder achtblättrige Goldblume auch den auferstandenen inneren Menschen.
Öl, 1961

14
THE HIDDEN POWER

This secret ruler reminds one of the hunchback in "Coming Up" (plate 5), but now he has revealed his greater, divine aspect. Invulnerable in his heavy armour, he walks with heavy tread towards the left. Dwarfs and kabiri are the great symbols of creative power in the artist, the smith and the magician. The creative principle is an unyielding necessity, but the same figure emanates light, and its head and shoulders contain the form of an egg – a germ of new life. The armour is finely wrought, for creativity seeks perfection of form.
Oil, May-June 1964

14
DER GEHEIME HERRSCHER

Dieser Herrscher erinnert an den Buckligen vom Bild «Der Aufsteigende» (Abb. 5); aber nun hat sich seine grössere, göttliche Seite offenbart. Unbesieglich in seinem harten Panzer, schreitet er mit schweren Schritten nach links. Zwerge, Kabiren sind die grossen Symbolgestalten des Schöpferischen, der Künstler, Schmiede und Zauberer. Das Schöpferische ist ein «eherner Zwang», aber die Figur strahlt ein Licht aus, und Kopf und Oberkörper sind wie in einem Ei enthalten, einem Keimbehälter neuen Lebens. Der Panzer ist feinste Arbeit; denn das Schöpferische sucht, sich in vollendeten Formen zu manifestieren.
Öl, Mai-Juni 1964

15
MOIRA

The anima (the female soul) of a man is also his fate, an ageless pattern that is mirrored in every mother, wife and lover. "It belongs to him, this perilous image of Woman; she stands for the loyalty which in the interests of life he must sometimes forgo; she is the much needed compensation for the risks, struggles and sacrifices that all end in disappointment; she is the solace for all the bitterness of life. And, at the same time, she is the great illusionist, the seductress, who draws him into life with her Maya [...] Because she is his greatest danger she demands from man his greatest, and if he has it in him, she will receive it." (C. G. Jung: *Aion*, CW 9/2, § 24.) In the picture she looks towards the left, towards the unconscious, and her hair (involuntary thoughts) has the green colour of vegetation. It forms (according to a dream) a bed in which 'her man' can rest.
Oil, 1965

15
MOIRA

Die Anima (weibliche Seele) des Mannes ist sein Schicksal; ein altersloses Bild, das sich in jeder Mutter, Gattin und Geliebten widerspiegelt. «Sie gehört zu ihm, sie ist die Treue, die er, gegebenenfalls um des Lebens willen, nicht immer haben darf. Sie ist die unumgängliche Kompensation für Wagnisse, Anstrengungen, Opfer, die alle mit Enttäuschung enden; sie ist die Trösterin gegenüber all der Bitternis des Lebens, und zugleich ist sie die grosse illusionserregende Verführerin zu eben diesem Leben. [...] Als seine grösste Gefahr fordert sie Grösstes vom Manne, und wenn er ein solcher ist, erhält sie es auch.» (C. G. Jung: *Aion*, GW 9/2, § 24.) Die grünen Haare, Gedanken, der Anima bereiten hier (nach einem Traum) ein Lager für ihren Mann.
Öl, 1965

16
AT THE DOOR

The painter also called the picture 'bull-man'. The divine creative power comes to the painter at night out of cosmic space, wanting to generate and form. But the nervous artist has locked the door; he is afraid of the strength of his uncanny visitor. The latter, however, actually brings light and life, as opposed to the narrow space where the artist has been living, unwilling to have contact with creativity.
Oil, August-September 1965

16
AN DER TÜR

Der Maler nannte das Bild auch «Stiermann». Nachts kommt aus dem Weltall die göttliche Schöpferkraft zum Maler und will zeugen und gestalten. Ängstlich hat der Künstler die Tür geschlossen; er fürchtet sich vor der Wucht des Einbrechenden, der aber eigentlich Leben und Licht besitzt, im Gegensatz zum engen Raum dessen, der ohne Kontakt mit dem Schöpferischen leben will.
Öl, August-September 1965

17
WITH CHILD

While a firestorm sweeps over the earth, the immaterial anima prepares in the dark depths the birth of the 'new human being', the immortal self which transcends death.
Oil, January 1966

17
DER KEIM

Unstofflich, unsichtbar, in der dunklen Tiefe unter einer vom Feuersturm heimgesuchten Erde, gebiert die Anima den «neuen Menschen», welcher den Tod überdauert.
Öl, Januar 1966

18
ANIMA WITH CROWN OF LIGHT

What Carl Spitteler called "the Lady Soul" is a messenger bringing new light to a man. The blue radiance of the spirit shows on her head, whilst she looks inward. This radiance consists of many germs of light, for the self (spiritual totality) is both one and many. Gerhard Dorn, the alchemist, points out that by meditating on the image of God, "little by little he (the Adept) will come to see with his mental eye a number of sparks shining day by day and more and more and growing into such a great light that thereafter all things needful to him will be made known" (*De Speculativa Philosophia, Theatr. Alchemicum*, 1602, vol. I, p. 275).
Oil, September 1966

18
ANIMA MIT LICHTKRONE

Die «Herrin Seele» (Spitteler) ist eine Botin; sie überbringt dem Manne neues Licht. Wie eine Krone ist das blaue Licht des Geistes auf ihrem Kopf sichtbar, während sie selbst nach innen blickt. Das Licht ist aus vielen Lichtkeimen zusammengesetzt, denn das Selbst (die seelische Ganzheit) ist eines und vieles zugleich. Wenn der Alchemist über das innere Gottesbild meditiert, sagt Gerhard Dorn, «so wird er mit seinen geistigen Augen wahrnehmen, wie einige Funken mehr und mehr durchschimmern und zu einem grossen Licht anwachsen, dass in der Folgezeit alles bekannt wird, was ihm notwendig ist» (*De Speculativa Philosophia, Theatr. Alchemicum*, 1602, Bd. I, S. 275).
Öl, September 1966

19
THE OBSERVER

Before we know ourselves we are already 'known'. The self represents the kernel of the psyche and its totality, and it watches us like a superior observer, as "private protection, intimate understanding as an individual judge, an inexorable witness" (Apuleius: *De Deo Socratis*, chapter 16), allowing no self-deception. It is both subhuman and superhuman and sees things far beyond our conscious mind.
Oil, 1966 (see also lithograph on back cover)

19
DER BEOBACHTER

Bevor wir irgendetwas von uns selbst verstehen, sind wir schon «erkannt». Wie ein übergeordneter Beobachter wacht das Selbst (das Seelenkern und Ganzheit darstellt) über uns. Apuleius (*De Deo Socratis*, Kap. 16) nennt ihn «privaten Beschützer, intimsten Kenner, individuellen Richter, unabweisbaren Zeugen». Er duldet keine Selbsttäuschungen. Er ist unter- und übermenschlich und sieht, was unserem menschlichen Bewusstsein, fernliegt.
Öl, 1966 (vgl. Lithographie auf der Buchrückseite)

Birkhäuser

20
BEAR AT THE TREE OF LIGHT

The dark God (Lamentations, 3,10: "He lies in wait for me like a bear") longs for the fruit of the tree of light, human consciousness. The tree is an image of inner growth (individuation) and growing consciousness, during which we continually find 'illuminations'. Only if the bear finds no light does he become dangerous. In this he resembles the visitor "At the Door" (plate 16), so it now becomes clear what this visitor had wanted.
Oil pastel, 1968

20
BÄR AM LICHTERBAUM

Der dunkle Gott (Jesaia, Klagelieder, 3,10: «Er [Gott] hat auf mich gelauert wie ein Bär, wie ein Löwe im Verborgenen ...») sehnt sich nach den Früchten des Lichterbaumes, nach dem Licht des menschlichen Bewusstseins. Der Baum ist ein Bild des Selbstwerdungs- und Bewusstwerdungsprozesses, im Laufe dessen dem Menschen immer wieder Lichter aufgehen. Der Bär gleicht dem Stiermann («An der Tür», Abb. 16), und so offenbart sich nun eigentlich, was jener mit seinem Besuch gewollt hatte.
Ölkreide, 1968

21
TORTOISE MAN

The tortoise is considered in mythology to be an ancient spirit of the earth. In Jungian terms it represents the self, inner wholeness. It also personifies complete introversion. Its shell was used for divination by the ancient Chinese, who heated it up to read the future from the cracks. The tortoise man in the painting is facing to the left, that is to say towards the meaning of the unconscious. He is glowing with an inner fire, and his knowing eye suggests secret wisdom.
Oil pastel, ca. 1968

21
SCHILDKRÖTENMANN

In Jung'scher Sprache stellt dieses Wesen das Selbst, die innere Ganzheit dar. Die Schildkröte gilt als uralter Geist der Erde. Sie verkörpert auch völligste Introversion. Ihr gemusterter Panzer wurde in China zu Orakelzwecken verwendet, indem man ihn erhitzte und dann aus den Bruchlinien die Zukunft herauslas. Der Schildkrötenmann des Bildes weist nach links, das heisst auf die Bedeutung des Unbewussten. Er ist von Feuer durchglüht, und sein kluges Auge weist auf geheimes Wissen hin.
Ölkreide, etwa 1968

22
WINDOW ON ETERNITY

According to the alchemist Gerhard Dorn, whoever opens his soul to the spiritual "influx of the divine" receives the revivifying experience of a higher world order. A "spiracle of eternal life" or "window on eternity" opens up and gives the soul "an opportunity to escape from the stifling grip of a one-sided view of the world" (C. G. Jung: *Mysterium Coniunctionis*, CW 14, § 763). The artist has himself become part of this cosmic spirit, for it uses the hand of a mortal man in order to reveal its mysterious constellations.
Oil pastel, August 1970

22
FENSTER ZUR EWIGKEIT

Wer sich nach Ansicht des Alchemisten Gerhard Dorn dem «göttlichen Einfliessen» des Geistes in die Seele öffnet, empfängt die Erkenntnis einer höheren Weltordnung. Es öffnet sich ihm ein «Luftloch des ewigen Lebens» oder ein «Fenster zur Ewigkeit», wodurch die Seele belebt wird. Es ist ein Ausblick, der uns «von dem erstickenden Zugriff eines einseitigen Weltbildes erlöst» (C. G. Jung, *Mysterium Coniunctionis*, GW 14/2, § 418). Der Maler ist hier selber ein Stück dieses kosmischen Geistes, indem letzterer sich der Hand des sterblichen Menschen bedient, um seine geheimen Ordnungen abzubilden.
Ölkreide, August 1970

23
THE WHITE LADY

The 'white lady' is popularly considered a harbinger of death (thus the darkened eyes) and she brings the cup of suffering and transformation. Shortly after the painting of this picture, P. B.'s wife died suddenly. The delicate vessel is reminiscent of the Grail which provides truth and spiritual nourishment. The whole ghostly figure haloed with blue light seems to be outside the colourful realm of life.
Oil, March 1971

23
DIE WEISSE FRAU

Die «Weisse Frau» ist im Volksglauben eine Todeskünderin (daher die lichtlosen Augen), und sie bringt den Kelch der leidvollen Verwandlung. Kurz nach dem Malen dieses Bildes verlor P. B. seine Gattin durch den Tod. Das zarte Gefäss, das die Frau hält, erinnert an das Gralsgefäss, welches Wahrheit und geistige Nahrung spendet. Die ganze Gestalt ist dem Farbenspiel des Lebens entrückt und von einem geisterhaften blauen Licht umspielt.
Öl, März 1971

24

24 MARCH 1971

This is the date of the unexpected and sudden death of Sibylle Birkhäuser. Although the whole framework of life (the house) has been shattered by the lightning, a suggestion lies beyond that what appears to be senseless and accidental is in fact the work of a cosmic force with human characteristics, in other words that meaning could after all be found in such a tragedy.
Oil, 1971

24

DER 24. MÄRZ 1971

Das ist das Datum des unerwarteten, plötzlichen Todes von Sibylle Birkhäuser. Obwohl der ganze Lebensrahmen – das Haus – von einem Blitz zersprengt wurde, tauchte dahinter eine Ahnung auf, dass dieses sinnlos-zufällige Geschehen die Tat eines menschenähnlichen kosmischen Geistwesens sein, das heisst, dass doch auch ein Sinn in solchem Unglück gefunden werden könnte.
Öl, 1971

25
GOD'S FIRE

The creative person experiences the divine grace of being allowed to light their small torch at the fire of the Creator and thus bring light to their world. P. B. once dreamed that he was given this grace. The animal face in the fire, formed like an eight-petalled flower, signifies enlightenment and order in the chaos.
Oil, June-September 1974

25
GOTTESFEUER

Der schöpferische Mensch erfährt die Gnade, dass er eine kleine Fackel am grossen Feuer des Schöpfergottes anzünden darf und so seine Welt erhellen kann. P. B. träumte einmal, dass ihm diese Gnade geschenkt wurde. Das tierartige Gesicht im Feuer deutet auf Erhellung, Ordnung im Chaos hin, da es wie eine achtstrahlige Blume komponiert ist.
Öl, Juni-September 1974

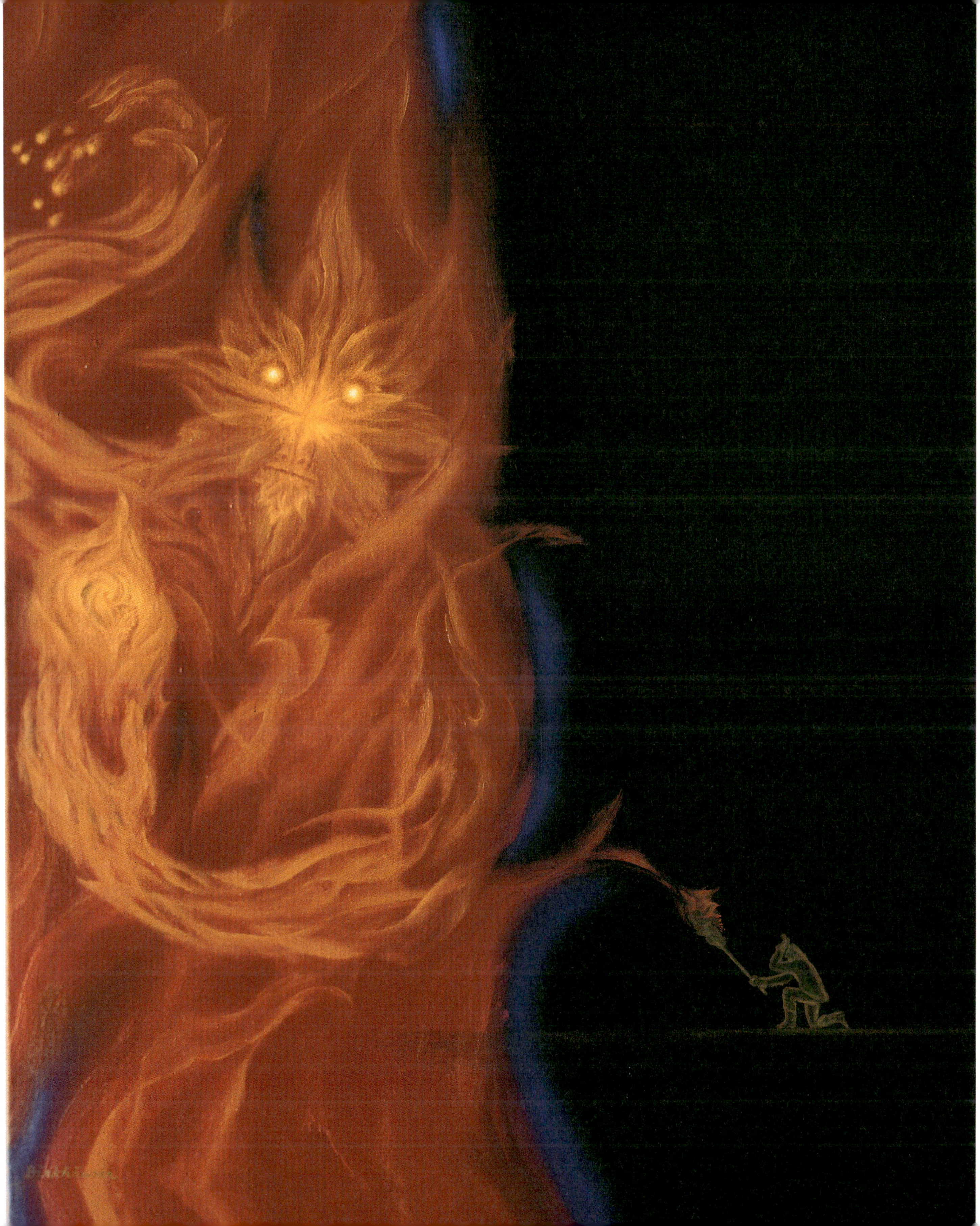

26
HAVING SPEECH

The split man of the "World's Wound" (plate 2) has been transformed by the artist's experience of the unconscious and by following its inspiration. Blood flows into the scar so that it could heal. The eyes look in the same direction and the man, formerly a despairing mute, now begins to speak.
Oil, April 1975

26
ZWIEGESPRÄCH

Durch die Hingabe an die Inspiration des Unbewussten und durch die Auseinandersetzung mit ihm ist der «Gespaltene» (Abb. 2) verwandelt. Seine Narbe wird durchblutet, so dass sie weiterheilen könnte. Die Augen blicken in gleicher Richtung, und der vorher Stumm-Verzweifelte beginnt zu sprechen.
Öl, April 1975

27
IN THE NIGHT OF 13 OCTOBER 1942

This is one of the few paintings which directly represents a dream. On 13 October 1942 Birkhäuser dreamed that he was climbing a steep, narrow ramp within the tower of Basel cathedral behind his wife. A miraculous being, half fish and half insect, climbed up beside the ramp on threads. At the top it turned into a fish's head, shining silvery in every colour. From its mouth emanated a blue light. Courageously, Sibylle Birkhäuser stood still; the fish approached her as if to kiss her and the blue light shone right through her. The dreamer went on and had to dare to jump from one platform to another on the opposite side of the abyss. From the platform an eye, the eye of God, was looking at him out of a green triangular frame. It penetrated him with its overwhelming light. This dream vision is the experience of 'vocation'. The anima is inspired and illumined before the artist himself.
Oil, September 1975

27
IN DER NACHT VOM 13. OKTOBER 1942

Eines der wenigen Bilder, das ein Traummotiv direkt wiedergibt. Birkhäuser träumte, er besteige hinter seiner Frau auf einer schmalen, steilen Rampe in dessen Innerem den einen Turm des Basler Münsters. Ein Wunderwesen, halb Fisch, halb Insekt, steigt bei der Rampe an Fäden empor und wird oben zu einem Fischkopf, der silbern und in allen Farben schimmert. Aus seinem Maul strahlt ein blaues Licht. Sibylle Birkhäuser bleibt mutig stehen; der Fisch nähert sich ihrem Gesicht, wie um sie zu küssen; sie wird von seinem blauen Glanz ganz durchstrahlt. Weitersteigend muss der Träumer einen grossen Sprung über den Abgrund auf eine gegenüberliegende Platte wagen. Von der Platte aus blickt ihn aus einem grünen dreieckigen Rahmen ein Auge an – das Auge Gottes! Es strahlt ein durchdringendes, überwältigendes Licht auf ihn. Diese Traumvision ist ein Berufungserlebnis. Die Anima wird vom Gottesgeist inspiriert und erleuchtet.
Öl, September 1975

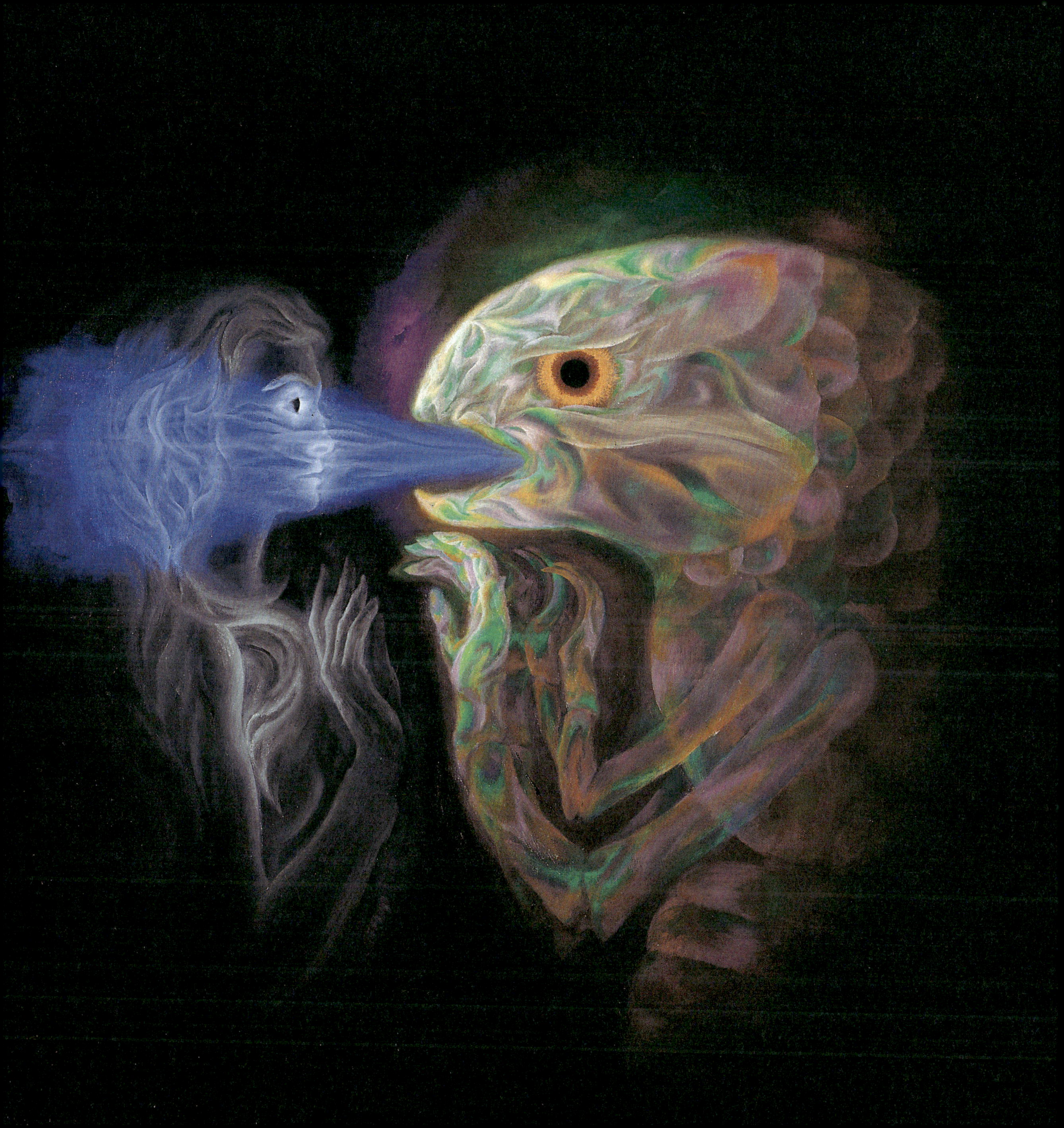

28

NATURE SPIRIT

P. B. kept dreaming of large and small wild cats and the aura of unselfconscious natural power emanating from them. We often believe they represent the animal instincts, but they also have a 'spirit' of their own, a way of seeing things in the light of the unconscious psyche. When they see, they project vision as well as registering an object. P. B.'s artistic eye was similar; it could project an image of the reality of the psyche.
Oil, June 1976

28

NATURGEIST

Immer wieder träumte Birkhäuser von grossen und kleinen Wildkatzen, von ihrer strahlenden, sorglosen Naturkraft. Wir glauben oft, sie stellten das Tierische, den Trieb dar, aber sie besitzen auch einen eigenen Geist, nämlich eine Art des Sehens, wie es dem Unbewussten eigen ist. Es ist ein Sehen, das Sicht aussendet, nicht nur empfängt. Das Künstlerauge P. B.s war von dieser Art, es «projizierte» (warf nach vorne) ein Bild von der Wirklichkeit der Seele.
Öl, Juni 1976

29
LYNX

The creative artist serves a spirit of nature which tries to manifest itself through him. But sometimes its enormous energy is too much for him, especially when the body becomes older. P. B. painted this picture, which is based on a dream, shortly before his death. The frail human being has to surrender to the powerful god. The lynx is a far-sighted creature which can see in the dark. Its name is related to *lux* (light).
Oil, September 1976

29
LUCHS

Der schöpferische Mensch dient einem Naturgeist, der sich durch ihn offenbaren will; doch manchmal sind dessen Energieballungen zu viel für den Menschen, besonders wenn sein Körper altert. Peter Birkhäuser malte dieses Bild, das auf einem Traum beruht, kurz vor seinem Tod. Der irdische Mensch muss sich der Übermacht des Gottes ergeben. Der Luchs ist der «Weitblickende», der auch im Dunkeln sieht. Sein Name hängt mit *lux* (Licht) zusammen.
Öl, September 1976

30

IN THE HANDS OF FATE / IN GOD'S HANDS

In antiquity the snake was worshipped as a god of time and eternity. It is the world spirit – incomprehensible, threatening and annihilating – but which also harbours a secret meaning. In its hands human beings are helpless, all the values of consciousness are overthrown (the man is upside down!). The spiky wavelike lines suggest cosmic waves or crystalline patterns in agate, like the 'secret patterns' which our lives follow.
Oil pastel 1967; Lithography 1975

30

IN DER HAND DES SCHICKSALS / IN GOTTES HAND

Die Schlange wurde in der Antike als Gott der Zeit und der Ewigkeit verehrt. Sie ist der Weltgeist, den wir nicht verstehen, der uns oft bedroht, am Ende vernichtet, und in dem doch ein verborgener Sinn wohnt. Der Mensch ist ihm hilflos ausgeliefert, als ob sich in seiner Gegenwart alle Bewusstseinswerte umkehren würden. Die zackigen Wellenlinien vermitteln ein Gefühl kosmischer Wellen oder kristalliner Bildungen im Achat – sie deuten auf ein Muster hin, dem unser Leben folgt.
Ölkreide 1967; Lithographie 1975

31
DUEL

If we look at our conflicts objectively (nirdvandva – free of the opposites) they reveal themselves as part of the very nature of the psyche, for the unconscious both does and does not want to enter into our consciousness. Here the more human-looking figure in the monk's habit of renunciation has the upper hand, since he has the weapon, a symbol of discrimination, which his opponent, the purely animal, lacks.
Oil pastel 1969; lithography 1973

31
ZWEIKAMPF

Wenn wir unsere Konflikte objektiv (nirdvandva – frei von Gegensätzen) betrachten, enthüllen sie sich als eine Eigenschaft des Unbewussten selber: es will und will doch auch nicht in uns bewusst werden. Der menschenähnliche Kämpfer in der Mönchstracht der Weltentsagung siegt, weil er die Waffe – ein Symbol des Unterscheiden- und Entscheidenkönnens – besitzt, die dem Nur-Tierischen fehlt.
Ölkreide 1969; Lithographie 1973

32

FOURFOLD FACE / FOUR-EYED WORLD SPIRIT

Quaternity, according to C. G. Jung, always points to inner totality. The spirit of the universe appears to us to be unconscious and animal-like, but also 'knowing' in a higher sense of the word. The spirit casts a dark shadow (the black sphere behind) and further back again a new sun is rising, perhaps the new light of a coming aeon which we will only see after passing through a great darkness.
Oil pastel 1969; lithography 1975

32

VIERÄUGIGER WELTGEIST

Vierheit weist nach C. G. Jung immer auf Ganzheit hin. Der Geist des Weltalls erscheint uns unbewusst-animalisch zu sein und in einem höheren Sinn «wissend» zugleich. Der Geist hat einen Schatten (die dunkle Kugel hinter ihm), und noch dahinter steigt eine neue Sonne empor, vielleicht das Licht eines kommenden Zeitalters, das wir erst sehen werden, wenn wir durch eine grosse Dunkelheit hindurchgegangen sind.
Ölkreide 1969; Lithographie 1975

33
STAR-WELL

This is a dream image. The coiled snake points to the centre. Among all the thousands of stars in the sky, folklore maintains that one is 'our star', meaning our individual destiny, which is the consummation of our totality. Every path and process of life (the snake) leads to that star, whether we know it or not. There, in the centre, is the wellspring of the 'water of life'.
Oil pastel 1970; lithography 1974

33
STERNBRUNNEN

Traummotiv. Die spiralig aufgerollte Schlange weist auf das Zentrum. Unter den vielen Sternen am Himmel ist nach dem Volksglauben einer «unser Stern», das individuelle Schicksal, in dem sich unsere Ganzheit verwirklicht. Jeder Lebensweg und Lebensprozess (die Schlange) führt dorthin, ob wir es wissen oder nicht. Dort, im Zentrum, ist der Brunnen, aus dem das Wasser des Lebens emporquillt.
Ölkreide 1970; Lithographie 1974

34
SPIRITUS ANIMALIS I

New apprehensions can be contained in what humans first regard as blind animal instincts, for the unconscious is both instinct and spirit. This bear, an ancient god image, has lights for eyes, it sheds illumination on the onlooker. On its forehead it has a third eye which can see the opposites together in one. The fur is like flames because this bear is a spirit, not a physical entity.
Lithography 1972

34
SPIRITUS ANIMALIS I

Was sich im Menschen zunächst als Trieb ankündigt, enthält neue Einsicht; denn das Unbewusste ist Instinkt und Geist zugleich. Der Bär – ein uraltes Gottesbild – hat Lichter statt Augen, er strahlt Erleuchtung auf den Beschauer. Auf der Stirn hat er ein drittes Auge, das die Weltgegensätze zusammenschauen kann. Der Pelz ist wie Flammen gestaltet, weil dieser Bär kein Körperwesen, sondern ein Geist ist.
Lithographie 1972

35
BUTTERFLY BIRTH

"The quickest horse that carries you to perfection is suffering" (Meister Eckhart). When the soul embraces and accepts suffering, the pain reveals itself as the birth pangs of a new inner being. 'Psyche' in classical Greek means 'soul' and 'butterfly'. The latter was a symbol of the soul led by Hermes after death flying into the beyond.
Oil pastel 1971; lithography 1976

35
SCHMETTERLINGSGEBURT

«Leiden ist das schnellste Pferd, das uns zur Vollendung trägt» (Meister Eckhart). Wenn die Seele das Leiden umarmt, entpuppt es sich als Geburtsschmerz eines neuen inneren Wesens. Das griechische Wort «Psyche» heisst Seele und Schmetterling. Letzterer ist ein Bild der Seele, wie sie nach dem Tode befreit, von Hermes geleitet, davonfliegt.
Ölkreide 1971; Lithographie 1976

36
THE FLAME DANCER

Now the anima – the 'Lady Soul' – has found her own real task: to mediate and bring to humans the divine fire and its creative power. Like the bearer of the Grail, or a Vestal Virgin, she guards the fire and also plays with it.
Oil 1974; lithography 1975

36
FEUERTÄNZERIN

Hier hat die Anima den Weg zu ihrer eigentlichen Aufgabe gefunden, als Vermittlerin des göttlichen Feuers, der schöpferischen Macht. Wie die Gralsträgerin oder wie die Vestalin hütet sie es und spielt auch zugleich mit ihm.
Öl 1974; Lithographie 1975

37
ISIS

The 'old woman' reveals her transcendent divine aspect. In the vision of 2nd century author Apuleius (*Metamorphoses* 11,3) she says about herself: "You see me here ... I am nature, the universal mother, mistress of all elements, primordial child of time, sovereign of all things spiritual, queen of the dead, queen of the immortals, the single manifestation of all gods and goddesses there are. My nod governs the shining heights of heaven, the wholesome sea breezes, the lamentable silences of the world below ..." Here she shows especially her aspect "as dread Prosperine to whom the owl cries at night, whose triple face is potent against the malice of ghosts".
Lithography, February 1976

37
ISIS

Die «Alte» offenbart ihre umfassendere göttliche Gestalt. In einer Vision des antiken Schriftstellers Apuleius (*Metamorphosen* 11,3) sagt sie von sich aus: «Du bist ich [...] die Mutter der Schöpfung, die Herrin der Elemente, der Urspross der Jahrhunderte, die höchste der Gottheiten, die Königin des Geistes, die Erste der Himmlischen, die Erscheinung der Götter und Göttinnen in einer Gestalt, die ich des Himmels lichtvolle Höhen, des Meeres wohltätiges Wehen, der Unterwelt vielbeweinte Stille durch meinen Wink leite.» Hier zeigt sie besonders Züge der «durch das nächtliche Geheul Schauder erregenden Proserpina», welche «den Ansturm der Geister bändigt».
Lithographie, Februar 1976

ANALYTICAL PSYCHOLOGY AND THE PROBLEMS OF ART

Peter Birkhäuser

Jung's discovery of suprapersonal, spontaneous spiritual activity in the unconscious has changed the way we need to see everything, even if outwardly this change is barely noticeable at the present time. As a result, Jung has enriched the most diverse fields of human intellectual and scientific endeavour, and it is still impossible to predict where and how far this innovation will lead in the future. In any event, it has shed new light on the problems of art. Indeed, I believe that Jung may have shown us the way leading out of the confusion in which art has lost its way.

Originally, figurative representation was a magic art, a charm to exorcise evil spirits, or a means to make the gods appear in visible form; a kind of religious ritual. It was a way of seeking healing and protection. For instance in Egyptian and classical antiquity, in the eastern civilizations, art was chiefly a religious instrument, and this was true as well in the Christian Middle Ages. As individuals artists remained anonymous. They were expected to stay in the background and accomplish most of their tasks along strictly prescribed and doctrinally predetermined lines.

The art of the Renaissance began to move away from this introverted attitude in which the *inner* image was the essential thing. It abandoned this previous source of inspiration, and as part of the general intellectual movement of the time it became extraverted. For many people the world of Christian ideas had lost its attraction and no longer provided adequate possibilities for expression. The new western *Zeitgeist* was outward-looking and fascinated by the secrets of nature, which had been ignored for so long. In art, too, attention began to focus on the rich panoply of external appearances. In those days, for instance, many artists were also scientists. One Renaissance painter wrote that he went to bed each night happy in the knowledge that next day he would be permitted to study 'the divine perspective'. Leonardo da Vinci excelled not only as a great artist, but also as an anatomist, mathematician and engineer; and Michelangelo was so fascinated by the structure of the human body that he devoted many years to its study.

Although paintings and statues for churches still formed the bulk of art produced at that time, the sacred images increasingly resembled attractive studies from nature. The human body with the play of muscles and the way it was posed in space, textile drapery, animals, plants and background landscapes became ever more important. At the same time, the original content, i. e. the Christian mythos, began to recede into the background. In their enthusiasm for pagan appreciation of the world, artists began to represent the gods of antiquity and their legends instead of their own. Soon afterwards, the Reformation was to batter a huge breach in the defences of dogmatic Christian traditions, giving it literal expression in the onslaught of the iconoclasts.

In his Bailey Island Seminar Jung said: "The Catholic Church is a way of living the unconscious, and the dogmas of the Catholic Church contain all the history of the unconscious objectified. Whatever they represent as happening is what happens in the unconscious."[1] As people increasingly departed from this inner world of images in the sixteenth century there arose a covert countercurrent: the symbolic fantasies of the alchemists. Jung discussed this in his Zarathustra Seminar[2], and he described the unbearable tensions caused by the loss of the sacraments of confession and absolution. For this reason, he said, the Wise Old Man came to the alchemists – here a personification of the unconscious – advising them to solve their problems through an inner priesthood, with the use of images, but the alchemists' introverted search and groping for a continued development of mythical conceptions found little resonance, apart from, for example, in Grünewald, Bosch or Dürer.

The sensitive barometer of art clearly indicates how the passion for representing the outer world continued to grow during the sixteenth and seventeenth centuries. There was no getting enough of the charms of the senses. The techniques of shading were added to perspective, in other words artists learned how to further emphasize spaciality and the curves of bodies through artful lighting and the principles of falling shadows. Anatomical features became fleshly – as with Rubens – and the sensuous pleasure in everything exter-

1 C. G. Jung, *Dream Symbols of the Individuation Process*. Seminar held at Bailey Island, Maine 1936 (private print). New: Suzanne Gieser (ed.), Philemon Foundation Series 15, Princeton & Woodstock: Princeton University Press, 2019, p. 125.

2 C. G. Jung, Seminars Vol 2 Part II: *Nietzsche's Zarathustra*: Notes of the Seminar Given 1934-39, p. 1351 (private print). New: James L. Jarret (ed.), London: Routledge & Kegan Paul, 1989, p. 320.

nal can be seen in countless beautiful still lifes of venison, set tables, fruit, fish, flowers, musical instruments, and so on. Some painters even specialized in portraying farmyard poultry! Motifs included domestic, society and military scenes, and portraiture played an increasingly important role. Subjects for artists also extended beyond the immediate surroundings of individuals to townscapes, seascapes or landscapes in the different seasons. The inner landscape, on the other hand, was increasingly lost from view. If the inner world was portrayed at all, it was in the form of traditional, emotionless church art in which the symbolism was in danger of being stifled by excessive materiality, or sought refuge in the alien context of classical mythology. The movement away from symbolic motifs and towards light can even be seen in a highly introverted and religious artist like Rembrandt.

Whereas in the seventeenth century the approach was still serious, weighty, at times naïve, what had started as a passionate attention to outer surfaces became superficiality in the eighteenth century. Elegance, *refinement* and sophisticated craftsmanship produced beautiful portraits, landscapes and the like, but the altar paintings of the time reveal how alienated they had become from their mythological sources. The Virgins are nothing more than saucy ladies, and the angels have all turned into cupids. True religious fervour, of the kind expressed in Gothic altar paintings, is nowhere to be found, because the energy of the images coming from the unconscious is lacking.

People in those days had largely lost touch with their inner being. A one-sidedly rational attitude predominated and with it a psychic rift and dissension that burst out in the French Revolution. The Revolution swept away a lot that was outdated and life-destroying, but it also led to the overestimation of human reason: in 1793, the *Déesse Raison* replaced the Virgin Mary in Notre Dame Cathedral in Paris and – in a fateful development – the 'cult of reason' was introduced.

Soon after that, Shelley, with considerable perspicacity, wrote that cultivation of the natural sciences, which had given humans mastery over the external world, demanded a corresponding expansion of the inner world to prevent the human race, which had made slaves of the elements, from becoming slaves themselves.

The Swiss artist Fuseli, too, painted a prophetic vision of the psychic state of the age: it portrays a sleeping woman extended in an excruciating posture with the nightmare imp pressing down on her chest. The huge, wild head of a blind mare can be seen behind her bed. The painting intimates that the mind, in the absence of the conscious faculties, is tormented by evil dreams and threatened by the blind frenzy of the unconscious. Prints of the painting were distributed widely in the years after the Revolution, but it was so poorly understood that it was sold in France accompanied by an obscene poem. The Revolution ended in a bloodbath and the megalomania of Napoleon. A relationship with the psyche was further away than ever.

It was a time of rather stagey art, a bloodless imitation of antiquity. David, a Jacobin painter and something of a propaganda minister for the revolutionary government, even wanted to force everyone to dress like ancient Romans! David wrote to a pupil he was encouraging to paint: "Vite, vite! Feuilletez votre Plutarque!" He was being urged to read the classics to find his subjects.

An opposing current began to flow in art during the German Romantic movement, but it was too weak and lacked the necessary armoury to overcome the materialistic bias against the spiritual. For example, the 'Nazarene' school took refuge in regressing into a kind of monastic existence, by trying to imitate the piety and inwardness of the Middle Ages; they painted altarpieces in the style of the 15th century, an attempt that was, of course, doomed to failure.

The single most daring and thoroughly positive attempt to find a way beyond the growth of rationalism is the magnificent landscapes of Caspar David Friedrich, in which he sought to represent the divine in nature. But he remained alone and misunderstood. When he died in 1840, art had on the whole become petrified in photographic imitation of the external world and in lifeless copies of former styles.

Goethe's Faust fantasy rears up like an isolated mountain range above the flat rationalism of his epoch. When he was asked reproachfully how on earth it was to be understood, he answered: "The more a poetic creation is incongruous and inaccessible to reason, the better it is!"[3]

In the light of the general attitude of utilitarianism and the one-sided preponderance of rationalism, the irrational found fewer and fewer outlets for expression, as even the religious forms had no life left in them. The soul remained banished to the underworld. However, since the powers of the unconscious could not be magicked away, they began to undermine the walls of reason from within. In art, a reaction set in against the still predominant ideals of the Renaissance, which had become tired and lifeless; around 1860, the Impressionists made their appearance. *Impressionism* is an inaccurate label which happened to to

3 *Conversation with Eckermann*, 6 May 1827.

be taken up because one of the paintings in an exhibition was entitled 'Impression'. They themselves used the name *Divisionistes,* because they divided up the phenomena of the visible world into their separate colour components. One group of *Divisionistes* even called themselves *Pointillistes,* because they used a matrix of coloured dots to create an image. The Impressionists emphasized their lack of interest in the content of paintings; they were far more concerned with the limited province of colour. This process of dismemberment went further with the advent of Cubism at the turn of the twentieth century, breaking down the forms of exterior phenomena into their basic geometrical elements. From there it was only a short step to abstract art, which renounced portrayal of both outer and inner objects. So by approximately the time of the First World War, the integral ideal representation of the outer world along traditional lines had disintegrated.

The outline given here naturally involves a lot of generalization and in reality diverse currents were running side by side and overlapping. The essence of the process, according to Jung, was the devaluation of the object. Art compensates for the bias of an age.

Another factor that contributed to the devaluation of an art that had become over-extraverted was the advent of photography. As an even more mechanical visual medium combined with a capacity for mass reproduction, photography dealt the deathblow to a naturalist style of painting completely devoid of spiritual vitality. Now that portrayals of the external world had been devalued and dissolved, the way had become clear for a turn to the image within. Without this development, it would never have been possible for art to free itself from the antiquated Renaissance ideal. We can see this in 19th century artists who tackled motifs from the interior world using traditional techniques, like Klinger, Böcklin or Thoma. Their paintings remained trapped in allegories, which were represented just like concrete outer reality.

When the pioneers of modern art turned away from externality it was a hopeful, promising development. But would they be able to access the world within? Was that even possible without a positive attitude to the psyche? Simply turning away from the exterior does not guarantee attention to the interior. Indeed, the unbroken supremacy of materialism with its devaluation of all things spiritual, which had been carried over from the 19th century, was in no mood to do so. It blocked the passage to the interior world.

In his Zarathustra Seminar Jung described how access to the unconscious is obstructed in the modern age, so that it forces its way to the surface and spews out inchoate lava. This kind of volcanic activity can be observed in a number of recent trends in art like Tachism with its portrayal of the unformed and shapeless. The violent eruption can be seen in the technique of firing a gun at a pot of paint, splattering its contents on the canvas, or pouring petrol on the painted surface and lighting it, so that the fire scorches out holes and bizarre patterns.

Randomly generated images like this may well have a stimulating effect on the imagination, but they will certainly not be enough on their own to express the contents of the unconscious, for the simple reason that we often experience very impressive, clearly defined and entire figures in dreams and fantasies, which act out scenes and dramatic events marked by their richness and exoticism. In his Dream Analysis Seminar Jung said: "One is impressed by the fact that the unconscious of man is a sort of mirror of great things."[4] However, all too frequently materialistic prejudices, cynicism and anxiety block access to the interior world, and the most widely disseminated psychologies are incapable of seeing its hidden values or else they consider them to be substitutes for sexuality and the like. The spirit cannot flourish under such influences.

These attitudes produced a dangerous state of explosive inner tensions because the collective unconscious had no effective connection to life. There will be "a great mental upheaval", Jung predicted decades ago, for this very reason, and it seems to us that this is precisely the state we have arrived at.[5]

We often hear people say that today's chaotic art is a representation of precisely this type of chaotic state, but being swamped by chaos is not the same thing as representing it. That would require detachment, a stable external conscious position from which to make a formative intervention. Besides, there is something negative about merely hanging around in a state of derangement. I believe the task is to search instead within this amorphous mass of 'chaotic lava' for signs of a new order. There is already a great unspoken longing to move beyond disintegration. With the right attitude it is possible to navigate the stream of the unconscious without losing one's own position; that is the only way to recognize and grasp what is valuable. The upsurge of psychic material must be scrutinized and selected, just as dreams would be meaningless without a conscious ego to experience them.

---

4 C. G. Jung, *Dream Analysis*. Notes of the Seminar Given in 1928-30, p. 447. William McGuire (ed.), London: Routledge & Kegan Paul, 1984, p. 447.

5 C. G. Jung, *Visions*. Notes of the Seminar Given in 1930-1934, 3. Claire Douglas (ed.), London: Routledge, 1998, p. 1352.

In his Zarathustra Seminar Jung described the great peril many people find themselves in owing to the loss of religion, the loss of contact with the depths of the unconscious, as follows: "That is what people don't know: they don't know that they are exposed naked to the unconscious when they can no longer use the old ways … They are defenceless and have to repress their unconscious, they cannot express it because it is inexpressible …"[6] The unconscious has become inexpressible for those who have barricaded all avenues leading to it because they are trapped in rationalism.

So there is good reason for the artists of today to seek access to the world within, to become some kind of safety-valve or container to hold what is surging up from below, on behalf of themselves and the rest of humanity. They need to try to harness the psychic powers in visual form, which will involve the realization that they are faced with something living and autonomous emerging from the psyche. Today's artists would thus do well to find some access to the inner world both for themselves and for their contemporaries, to provide a valve, or to be a vessel that can receive the contents of the unconscious. They should try to capture the psychic forces in pictures. This implies that they must have experienced them as being alive and spontaneous.

For instance, a giant wild huntsman dressed in green – a figure resembling Odin – came to a painter in a dream, forcing his way into the studio and demanding to be painted, a clear manifestation of the spontaneous activity of figures in the unconscious seeking out an individual in order to be seen and recorded. Another dream involved a person in an endless, labyrinthine cave system. He knew something else lived there which was looking for him: a mighty figure, half beast, half god. He was terrified of this being and ran away from it, yet was attracted by it at the same time. This was an image of the creative daemon of the unconscious, hungry for contact with the human being, pursuing him over long and twisting paths. This is the equivalent of Pollux, the immortal, divine brother of the Dioscuri.

This is a power which can also turn into a destructive demon if it continues to be denied and excluded from life. A talented man who was, however, liable to misuse unconscious contents for selfish ends, dreamed of someone who had discovered a huge, ancient, underground vault filled with golden honey. He forced his way in and opened the doors, letting the honey escape in such a rush that the greedy man drowned in it. Then the dreamer

6 C. G. Jung, Seminars Vol 2 Part I: *Nietzsche's Zarathustra*: Notes of the Seminar Given 1934-39, James L. Jarret (ed.), London: Routledge & Kegan Paul, 1989, p. 311.

himself climbed down into the vault to retrieve the spoils, but was ambushed by the devil and only escaped by the skin of his teeth. This dream shows how the treasure in the unconscious can prove a bane; its misuse may summon the devil.

It is really impressive to see how the unconscious reacts to these problems and responds according to each individual case. In dreams it sheds light on situations that are frequently obscure to consciousness, at times inspiring, encouraging, supportive, at others critical, admonitory or censorious.

A woman who was about to start a creative project and needed encouragement had a dream that her garden was full of ripe, golden apples. Being productive is here envisaged as harvesting something valuable that has ripened in the unconscious. By contrast someone else who was avoiding an intellectual activity dreamed that the fruit in a garden was rotting because it hadn't been picked. A man who was still totally unaware of his intellectual capacities dreamed that he had discovered a wonderful, exotic, richly decorated treasure chest. Indeed, a dream motif that appears regularly is the big house with unexplored rooms full of precious things. A woman who had spent a long time in analysis and then became an analyst herself had dreamed many years previously that she had found a healing spring in a subterranean cave which required years of patient work to encase for use. Someone working on a creative writing project had made the mistake of treating a serious subject ironically. In his dream a great female artist, a painter of mythical fantasies, had died as a result of cynical comments written about her paintings. This dream made the writer realize that the artistic woman inside him would die if his conscious mind failed to treat the images from his unconscious seriously.

All the dream images I have just described are a clear indication of how the ego is the recipient of powerful, superior and valuable elements which may be present in the unconscious. They also reveal that the ego requires the appropriate attitude of humility in order to gain access to these treasures and must be willing to accept tribulations and sacrifices, in the same way the hero in fairy tales has to take on an inferior role. He must sacrifice all sense of entitlement and often has to carry out difficult and dangerous tasks before obtaining the hoped-for prize. So it might well be the task imposed on the artist of today to develop a new form of expression suited to the age which does justice to the contents of the unconscious. It involves a struggle to make things visible that almost defy representation. The more seriously painters take the inner images, the greater their wish to perfect their portrayal will be.

When modern art was forced to turn away from all traditions around the turn of the twentieth century, it also abandoned the traditional techniques of its craft. The inheritance of draughtsmanship, learnt with much painstaking study of figurative drawing, perspective and so on was not a problem in itself; what had to be rejected was the way it had been abused in the naturalistic art of the 19th century. It could seem questionable to abandon all these inherited riches of knowledge and skill, and yet there was no avoiding the fact that it was the means of expression of an art which had become more and more one-sidedly extravert – excessively scientific – in order to capture every single detail of outward appearance. What is dangerous about these classical techniques is that objects from the interior world portrayed like this could be drawn too far in a material direction and thus distorted. On the other hand it does not seem to be a satisfactory solution to be content with the random and amorphous products of dripped paint I have described as modern art either. That would be rather like accepting a found object like a quaintly twisted tree-root as an adequate expression of the unconscious. Stimulating the imagination in this way is probably the basis – rather like the *prima materia* – from which the value must then be distilled in painstaking labour.

From what I have been trying to sketch out so far it should be clear that art today is no longer a mere matter of aesthetics. It is not an end in itself according to the motto 'art for art's sake' but should be seen as an aid to finding ways of expressing new, undiscovered psychic contents. The ego must behave in a receptive way, which requires a religious attitude – religious in the sense of carefully observing and taking account of psychic factors. Whereas religious art in former times produced paintings of generally sanctioned and orthodox subjects, today's artists are on their own with their experiences, exposed to all types of error. In *Psychology and Religion* Jung wrote: "A dogma is always the result and fruit of many minds and many centuries, purified of all the oddities, shortcomings, and flaws of individual experience. But for all that, the individual experience, by its very poverty, is immediate life, the warm red blood pulsating today. It is more convincing to a seeker after truth than the best tradition."[7] This sort of individual experience implies a return to a kind of primal condition, since it is individual visions that reveal the world within. It is a new beginning.

7 C. G. Jung, *Psychology and Religion*, CW 11, § 88.

Jung saw himself primarily as a physician, but it has become increasingly clear that he did not just treat individual patients but became a healer of his entire age. By helping countless people to relate to the productive, guiding and structuring side of the psyche, he provided a wider context to the problem of psychological suffering, showing that it was a result of being disconnected from one's essential being and true destiny. By pointing this out, he freed people of our time from the bleak and futile restrictiveness of a materialist world view and gave them the opportunity to experience the workings of the mysterious powers that give individual meaning to their lives.

The psychic life cannot thrive in an atmosphere of rationalism, which lies like a stone on top of a plant, smothering any idiosyncratic creative seed that tries to germinate and develop in the psyche. Jung freed it from this encumbrance. He not only gave a theoretical delineation of this spiritual urge in the unconscious; he also showed examples of how it operates and let it inform his own life.

For this reason artists today can see Jung as a role model in the search for a path to the treasure-house of the soul. Speaking of that precious vessel he gave us the beautiful and comforting words: "It seems to me that nothing essential has ever been lost, because its matrix is ever-present within us and from this it can and will be reproduced if needed."[8]

Zürich, 6 June 1970, on the occasion of the memorial ceremony for C. G. Jung

8 C. G. Jung, *Letters* Volume 2, letter of 14 September 1960 to Miguel Serrano. Princeton: Princeton University Press, 1975, p. 595.

ANALYTISCHE PSYCHOLOGIE UND DIE PROBLEME DER KUNST

Peter Birkhäuser

Jung hat durch seine Entdeckung einer überpersönlichen, unabhängigen geistigen Tätigkeit im Unbewussten gewissermassen allem ein anderes Vorzeichen gegeben, wenn dies auch an der Oberfläche unserer Zeit noch wenig sichtbar sein mag. Er hat damit die verschiedensten Gebiete der Geistes- und Naturwissenschaften befruchtet, und es ist noch gar nicht abzusehen, wie weit und wohin diese Erneuerung in Zukunft dringen wird. So ist durch ihn auch neues Licht gefallen auf die Probleme der Kunst. Ja, ich glaube, dass er den Weg gezeigt hat, der aus dem Chaos herausführt, in dem die Kunst sich verloren hat. Ursprünglich war das bildliche Darstellen etwas Magisches, ein Zauber, um Geister zu bannen, oder ein Mittel, Götter sichtbar zu machen; eine Art von Gottesdienst. Man suchte sich zu heilen und zu schützen damit. So war im alten Ägypten, im klassischen Altertum und in den östlichen Kulturen die Kunst vor allem ein religiöses Werkzeug, wie auch noch im christlichen Mittelalter. Der Künstler trat als Individuum kaum in Erscheinung; er hatte zurückzustehen und die meistens genau vorgeschriebene, dogmatisch festgelegte Aufgabe zu erfüllen.

Von dieser introvertierten Haltung, in der das *innere* Bild das Wesentliche war, begann sich die Kunst der Renaissance hinwegzubewegen. Sie kehrte sich von jener Quelle der Inspiration ab und ging als ein Teil der allgemeinen grossen Geistes-Strömung jener Zeit auf die Extraversion zu. Die Welt der christlichen Vorstellungen hatte für viele an Anziehungskraft und an Ausdrucksmöglichkeit verloren, und der veränderte abendländische Geist wandte sich nach aussen, fasziniert von den Geheimnissen der lange missachteten Natur. Auch in der Kunst floss das Interesse dem ganzen Reichtum der äusseren Erscheinung zu. So waren manche der damaligen Künstler zugleich Naturwissenschafter. Ein Renaissance-Maler sagte, wenn er sich abends schlafen lege, so fühle er sich glücklich, weil er am nächsten Tage wieder die göttliche Perspektive studieren dürfe. Leonardo da Vinci zeichnete sich nicht nur als grosser Künstler aus, sondern auch als Anatom, Mathematiker und Techniker. Und Michelangelo war so fasziniert vom Bau des menschlichen Körpers, dass er viele Jahre an dessen Studium wandte. Obwohl man noch meistens Gemälde und Statuen für Kirchen schuf, näherten sich die heiligen Bilder mehr und mehr schönen Naturstudien an. Der menschliche Körper mit seiner Muskulatur und seinen Stellungen im Raum, Faltenwürfe, Tiere, Pflanzen und die Landschaften des Hintergrundes wurden immer wesentlicher. Der ursprüngliche Inhalt, der christliche Mythos, begann daneben zurückzutreten. Begeistert von heidnischer Weltlust, stellte man antike Götter und ihre Sagen dar anstelle der eigenen. Bald sollte dazu noch die Reformation eine gewaltige Bresche in die Welt der christlichen dogmatischen Vorstellungen schlagen und diesen Angriff handgreiflich mit den Bilderstürmen verwirklichen.

Im Seminar von Bailey Island sagte Jung: «Die katholische Kirche ist eine Art, das Unbewusste zu leben, und die Dogmen der katholischen Kirche enthalten objektiviert all die Geschichte des Unbewussten. Was immer sie auch repräsentieren und was geschieht, ist das, was im Unbewussten geschieht.»[1] Die zunehmende Abwendung von jener inneren Bilderwelt im 16. Jahrhundert brachte eine geheime Gegenströmung an die Oberfläche: die symbolischen Phantasien der Alchemisten. Jung spricht hierüber im Zarathustra-Seminar und beschreibt die unerträgliche Spannung, welche entstanden sei durch den Verlust der Confessio und der Absolution.[2] Deshalb sei zu den Alchemisten der weise alte Mann gekommen – hier eine Personifikation des Unbewussten – und habe ihnen geraten, sie sollten Bilder machen, um ihre Probleme durch die innere Priesterschaft zu lösen. Das introvertierte Suchen der Alchemisten und ihr Tasten nach einer Weiterentwicklung der mythischen Vorstellungen hatte jedoch im allgemeinen wenig Nachfolge gefunden. Ausnahmen waren zum Beispiel Grünewald, Bosch und Dürer.

Das empfindliche Barometer der Kunst zeigt nun deutlich, wie im Laufe des 16. Jahrhunderts und im 17. die Leidenschaft für die Darstellung des Äussern noch mehr zugenommen hatte. Man konnte sich kaum mehr sättigen an all den stofflichen Reizen. Zur Perspektive war die Schattenlehre getreten, das heisst, man lernte, durch kunstvolle Führung der Beleuchtung und den gesetzmässigen Schattenwurf die Räumlichkeit und Rundung der Körper noch mehr hervorzuheben. Das Anatomische wurde zum Fleischlichen – wie

1 C.G. Jung, *Dream Symbols of the Individuation Process*. Seminar held at Bailey Island, Maine 1936 (Privatdruck). Neu herausgegeben von Suzanne Gieser. Philemon Foundation Series, 15, 2019

2 C.G. Jung, *Nietzsche's Zarathustra*: Notes of the Seminar Given 1934-39, S. 1351. Neu herausgegeben von James L. Jarret, Routledge & Kegan Paul, 1989, S. 320.

etwa bei Rubens –, und die sinnliche Freude an allem Äussern, Gegenständlichen schlug sich nieder in zahllosen schönen Stillleben von Wildbret, gedeckten Tischen, Früchten, Fischen, Blumen, Musikinstrumenten usw. Es gab sogar Spezialisten für die Darstellung von Hühnerhöfen! Häusliche, gesellschaftliche und militärische Szenen wurden zum Thema, und das Porträt spielte eine immer grössere Rolle. Auch die weitere Umgebung des Menschen rückte in das Blickfeld: Städte- und Marinebilder oder Landschaften in den verschiedenen Jahreszeiten. Aber die innere Landschaft verschwand mehr und mehr. Malte man innere Gegenstände, dann waren es kühle, traditionelle Kirchenbilder, deren übertriebene Stofflichkeit den symbolischen Inhalt zu verdecken droht, oder man flüchtete sich in das fremde Gebiet antiker Mythen. Sogar bei einem so introvertierten und religiösen Künstler wie Rembrandt bewegte sich die Betonung vom symbolischen Thema weg und auf das Licht zu. Während im 17. Jahrhundert noch alles ernsthaft, schwer und zuweilen naiv war, wurde im 18. jene ursprünglich leidenschaftliche Zuwendung zum Äussern zur Äusserlichkeit. Eleganz, Raffiniertheit und ein zum höchsten entwickeltes Handwerk brachten zwar wunderschöne Bildnisse, Szenerien und dergleichen hervor, aber ein Altarbild jener Epoche enthüllt die Abgeschnittenheit vom mythischen Hintergrund. Diese Marien sind bloss noch pikante Damen, und die Engel werden zu Amoretten. Nirgends mehr ist eine Ergriffenheit zu spüren wie etwa im Ausdruck eines gotischen Altarbildes. Die Stosskraft der Bilder aus dem Unbewussten ist daraus verschwunden. Die Menschen jener Zeit hatten schon weitgehend den Kontakt mit der inneren Welt verloren. Die Einseitigkeit einer rationalistischen Einstellung wuchs und damit die seelische Spaltung und Spannung, welche sich dann in der gewaltigen Explosion der Französischen Revolution Luft machte. Viel Überholtes und Lebenswidriges wurde davon weggesprengt, aber auch der Weg freigelegt für eine Überschätzung der menschlichen Vernunft: 1793 wurde die *Déesse Raison* in der Notre Dame zu Paris an die Stelle Marias gesetzt und ein «Kultus der Vernunft» eingeführt. – Ein schicksalhafter Augenblick!

Bald danach schrieb Shelley weitblickend, die Pflege der Naturwissenschaften, welche die Herrschaft des Menschen über die äussere Welt gebracht, erfordere eine entsprechende Ausdehnung der innern Welt, damit der Mensch, der die Elemente zu Sklaven gemacht, nicht selbst zum Sklaven werde. Und der Zürcher Künstler Johann Heinrich Füssli malte damals ein Bild, das die seelische Situation der Zeit in prophetischer Schau erfasste: Eine schlafende Frau, in gequälter Stellung liegend, auf deren Brust ein Nachtmahr sitzt. Hinter ihrem Bett erscheint der wilde, riesige Kopf eines blinden Pferdes. Das Bild deutet an, wie die Seele, bewusstlos, von bösem Traum gequält und von der blinden Raserei des Unbewussten bedroht ist. Dieses Gemälde war als Kupferstich in den Revolutionsjahren sehr verbreitet, aber man begriff es so wenig, dass es in Frankreich mit einem daruntergesetzten obszönen Gedicht verkauft wurde. Die Revolution führte dann zu einem Blutbad und zum Machtrausch Napoleons. Man war weiter als je von einer Beziehung zur Seele entfernt.

Die Kunst dieser Zeit nahm etwas Kulissenhaftes an, ein kaltes Nachahmen des Altertums. Der jakobinische Maler David, eine Art von Propagandaminister in der Revolutionsregierung, wollte sogar einmal erzwingen, dass jedermann altrömische Kleider trage! Und David schrieb einem Schüler, den er zum Malen anregen wollte: «Vite, vite! Feuilletez votre Plutarque!» Der Schüler musste also in einem Buch des Altertums nachlesen, was er zu malen hatte.

In der Kunst der deutschen Romantik zeichnete sich eine Gegenbewegung ab, doch war sie zu schwach und besass noch nicht das geistige Rüstzeug, welches die Überwindung der materialistischen Vorurteile gegen das Seelische ermöglicht hätte. So flüchtete sich zum Beispiel die Künstlergruppe der Nazarener in eine Regression. Sie zog sich in eine Art von Klosterleben zurück, versuchte, mittelalterliche Frömmigkeit und Innerlichkeit nachzuempfinden, und malte Altarbilder, die denen des 15. Jahrhunderts glichen, ein Versuch, der natürlich zum Scheitern verurteilt war.

Ein einzelnes, kühnes, äusserst positives Unternehmen, das über den wachsenden Rationalismus hinausführte, war Caspar David Friedrichs geniale Landschaftsmalerei, in der er das Göttliche in der Natur darzustellen suchte. Aber er blieb allein und unverstanden. Als er 1840 starb, war die Kunst im allgemeinen bereits erstarrt in photographischem Nachahmen des Äussern und in leblosen Stilimitationen. Wie ein einsames Gebirge ragt Goethes Faust-Phantasie in jene vernunftgläubige Epoche hinein. Als man ihn vorwurfsvoll fragte, wie sie denn zu verstehen sei, antwortete er: «Je inkommensurabler und für den Verstand unfasslicher eine poetische Produktion, desto besser!»[3]

Dem allgemeinen Nützlichkeitsdenken und dem einseitigen Überwiegen des Verstandesmässigen entsprechend, fand das Irrationale immer weniger Ausdrucksmöglichkeit, denn auch die religiösen Formen waren allen Lebens bar. – Die Seele blieb in die Unterwelt verbannt. Da sich aber die Mächte des Unbewussten nicht wegzaubern liessen, begannen sie, das Gebäude der Vernunft von innen her zu unterhöhlen. In der Kunst

3 Johann Peter Eckermann: *Gespräche mit Goethe*, 6. Mai 1872

bildete sich eine Reaktion gegen das immer noch vorherrschende, alt und leblos gewordene Renaissance-Ideal: Um 1860 traten die Impressionisten auf. «Impressionismus» ist eine ganz uneigentliche Bezeichnung, die durch Zufall hängen blieb, weil ein ausgestelltes Bild «Impression» hiess. Sie selbst nannten sich «Divisionistes», da sie die Erscheinung der äussern Welt in ihre Farbelemente aufteilten. Eine Gruppe der Divisionistes nannte sich sogar «Pointillistes», weil sie ihre Darstellungen in rasterartige Farbpunkte auflösten. Die Impressionisten betonten ihre Uninteressiertheit am Inhalt der Bilder; wesentlich war ihnen das Teilgebiet der Farben. Dieser Zerlegungsprozess setzte sich weiter fort: Um die Wende zum 20. Jahrhundert erschien der Kubismus. Er löste Formen der äussern Erscheinung in ihre geometrischen Grundelemente auf. Von da war es nur ein Schritt zur abstrakten Kunst, die sich von äussern wie von innern Gegenständen losgesagt hat. Damit war ungefähr zur Zeit des Ersten Weltkrieges das traditionelle, ganzheitliche Idealbild der äussern Welt aufgelöst. Natürlich ist dieser Vorgang hier verallgemeinert und nur in den wichtigsten Hauptlinien beschrieben. In Wirklichkeit liefen vielerlei Strömungen nebeneinander her und überschnitten sich. Jung sagte von diesem Prozess, seine Essenz sei die Entwertung des Objekts. Die Kunst bilde ein Gegengewicht zur Tendenz eines Zeitalters.

Zur Entwertung einer zu extravertierten Kunst trug auch die Erfindung der Photographie bei. Diese noch mechanischere Abbildung des Äussern, zusammen mit ihrer maschinellen Massenhaftigkeit, gab der geistentleerten naturalistischen Malerei vollends den Todesstoss. Mit der Entwertung und Auflösung des Bildes der äussern Welt war der Weg freigelegt zum innern Bild. Ohne diese Entwicklung hätte man sich wohl nicht vom überlebten Renaissance-Ideal zu befreien vermocht. Dies ist zu beobachten bei Künstlern des 19. Jahrhunderts, die sich in traditioneller Weise mit inneren Motiven befassten, wie etwa Klinger, Böcklin oder Thoma. Ihre Malerei blieb in Allegorien befangen, welche ganz konkret, wie eine äussere Realität, dargestellt wurden.

Die Abwendung vom Äussern, welche die Pioniere der modernen Kunst hervorgebracht, war hoffnungsvoll und aussichtsreich. Aber konnte man nun den Zugang zum Innern finden? Kann man ihn finden, ohne eine positive Einstellung zur Psyche? Die Abwendung vom Äussern ist an sich noch keine Zuwendung zum Innern. Und die immer noch vorherrschende materialistische Einstellung aus dem 19. Jahrhundert mit ihrer Herabsetzung des Seelischen war wenig dazu angetan. Sie blockierte den Weg nach innen.

Im Zarathustra-Seminar beschrieb Jung, wie beim modernen Menschen die Zugänge zum Unbewussten verstopft seien, weshalb sich dieses mit Gewalt Luft mache und eine chaotische Lava herausschleudere. Dieser Ausbruch ist sichtbar geworden in verschiedenen Richtungen der neueren Kunst, wie zum Beispiel im Tachismus, der das noch Ungeformte, Gestaltlose abbildet. Das vulkanisch-gewaltsame Herausschleudern zeigt sich in jenem Verfahren, wo mit dem Gewehr auf gefüllte Farbgefässe geschossen wird, die dann ihren Inhalt auf die Leinwand verspritzen. Oder es werden aufgetragene Farbmassen mit Benzin übergossen und angezündet, worauf das Feuer Löcher und bizarre Formen herausbrennt.

Solche, nach den Gesetzen des Zufalls entstandenen Bildungen mögen anregend sein für die Phantasie, doch können sie kaum allein genügen, um die Inhalte des Unbewussten auszudrücken. Dies aus dem ganz einfachen Grund, weil uns in Träumen und Phantasien oft sehr eindrucksvolle, ganzheitliche, deutlich ausgeformte Gestalten entgegentreten und sich in Szenerien, die durch Fremdartigkeit und grossen Reichtum ausgezeichnet sind, dramatische Handlungen ereignen. Jung sagte im Traum-Seminar: «Man ist beeindruckt von der Tatsache, dass das Unbewusste des Menschen eine Art Spiegel grosser Dinge ist.»[4] Aber materialistische Vorurteile, Zynismus und Angst verbauen den Zugang zum Innern nur zu oft, und die verbreitetsten Psychologien vermögen die darin verborgenen Werte nicht zu sehen oder betrachten sie als uneigentliche Sexualität und dergleichen; ein Einfluss, unter dem das Seelische nicht gedeihen kann.

Durch solche Haltungen entstand ein gefährlicher Zustand explosiver innerer Spannungen, indem das kollektive Unbewusste nirgends mehr richtig an das Leben angeschlossen war. «Es wird eine weltweite Umwälzung geben», prophezeite Jung aus diesem Grunde schon vor Jahrzehnten, und es scheint uns, wir seien bereits mitten in diesem Zustand angelangt.[5]

Oft hört man, das Chaos der heutigen Kunst sei ja eben gerade die Darstellung dieses innern chaotischen Zustandes. Aber selbst im Chaos zu versinken, ist keine Darstellung davon.

Dafür braucht es Abstand, einen festen Standpunkt des Bewusstseins ausserhalb und ein gestaltendes Eingreifen. Zudem ist das passive Verharren in der Auflösung etwas zu Negatives. Die Aufgabe bestünde, meines Erachtens, eher darin, in dieser formlosen Masse der chaotischen Lava die Anzeichen einer neuen Ordnung zu suchen. Insgeheim herrscht

4 C. G. Jung, *Dream Analysis.* Notes of the Seminar Given in 1928-30, p. 447. Ed. William Mc Guire, London, Routledge & Kegan Paul, 1984.

5 C. G. Jung, *Visions.* Notes of the Seminar Given in 1930-1934, 3. Ed. Claire Douglas, Bollingen Series XCIX, Princeton, 1967.

bereits eine grosse Sehnsucht, über das Auflösende hinauszugelangen. Bei richtiger Einstellung kann man sich von der Strömung des Unbewussten ergreifen lassen, ohne den eigenen Standpunkt zu verlieren; man kann das Wertvolle überhaupt nur so erkennen und festhalten. Das andringende geistige Material muss ja beobachtet und ausgewählt werden können. Was wäre ein Traum, wenn ihm kein wahrnehmendes, bewusstes Ich gegenüberstünde?

Die grosse Gefahr, in die viele Menschen geraten sind durch den Verlust der Religion, durch den Unterbruch einer Verbindung mit den Tiefen des Unbewussten, beschrieb Jung im Zarathustra-Seminar folgendermassen: «Das ist es, was die Leute nicht wissen: dass sie nackt dem Unbewussten ausgesetzt sind, wenn sie nicht länger mehr die alten Wege benützen können ... Sie sind schutzlos und müssen ihr Unbewusstes unterdrücken. Sie können es nicht ausdrücken, weil es unausdrückbar geworden ist ...»[6] Das Unbewusste ist unausdrückbar geworden für die im Rationalismus Gefangenen, welche sich alle Wege dazu verbaut haben.

Der heutige Künstler hat also allen Grund, für sich und seine Mitmenschen einen Zugang zum Innern zu suchen, gewissermassen ein Ventil zu bilden oder ein Gelass zu sein, um das von dort Andringende aufzunehmen. Er muss versuchen, die seelischen Mächte in Bilder zu fassen. Dazu gehört auch die Erfahrung, dass ihm aus der Psyche etwas Lebendiges, Selbständiges entgegentritt.

So träumte es einem Maler, ein riesiger wilder Jäger in grünem Kleide – eine Wotan ähnliche Gestalt – dringe in seine Werkstatt ein und verlange, gemalt zu werden. Hier stellt sich deutlich die selbständige Aktivität der Figuren des Unbewussten dar, wie sie den Menschen aufsuchen, um gesehen und festgehalten zu werden. Und jemandem träumte es, er befinde sich in einem endlosen, labyrinthisch verschlungenen Höhlensystem. Er wusste, dass darin auch ein anderer lebte, eine mächtige, halb tierisch, halb göttliche Gestalt, die *ihn* suchte. Er fürchtete sich vor diesem Wesen, floh vor ihm und war zugleich von ihm angezogen. Hier hat sich der schöpferische Dämon des Unbewussten abgebildet, wie er die Berührung mit dem Menschen begehrt, wie er ihn auf langen, verschlungenen Wegen verfolgt. Er ist wie der unsterbliche, göttliche Bruder beim Dioskurenpaar.

Diese Macht kann aber auch zum zerstörenden Dämon werden, wenn sie immer verleugnet und vom Leben ausgeschlossen wird. Ein begabter Mann, der aber in Gefahr

6 C. G. Jung, *Nietzsche's Zarathustra*: Notes of the Seminar Given 1934-39. Neu herausgegeben von James L. Jarret, S. 1249. Routledge & Kegan Paul, 1989

war, die Inhalte des Unbewussten zu egoistischen Zwecken zu benützen, träumte von jemandem, der ein riesiges, uraltes, unterirdisches Gewölbe entdeckt hatte, das ganz mit goldgelbem Honig gefüllt war. Er drang dort ein und öffnete das Tor, worauf der Honig mit solcher Wucht herausströmte, dass der Begierige darin ertrank. Der Träumer selbst stieg dann ebenfalls in den Raum hinab, um die Beute einzubringen, wurde aber dort vom Teufel überrascht und konnte sich nur durch einen Kampf auf Leben und Tod erretten. In diesem Traume zeigt sich, wie der im Unbewussten verborgene Wert auch zum Unheil werden kann. Die Möglichkeit des Missbrauchs ruft den Teufel auf den Plan.

Ausserordentlich eindrucksvoll ist es immer, wie das Unbewusste selbst zu diesen Problemen Stellung bezieht und auf den individuellen Fall abgestimmt reagiert. Im Traum schildert es die jeweilige Lage, die dem Bewusstsein oft so dunkel ist: einmal inspirierend, ermutigend, bestärkend, dann wieder kritisierend, warnend oder ablehnend.

Einer Frau, die vor einer schöpferischen Aufgabe stand und Ermutigung brauchte, träumte es, ihr Garten hänge voller reifer, goldfarbener Äpfel. Hier ist das Produzieren dargestellt als ein Ernten eines Wertvollen, das im Unbewussten herangereift ist. Umgekehrt träumte es jemandem, der sich vor seiner geistigen Aufgabe drückte, die Früchte seines Gartens verfaulten, weil er es versäume, sie zu pflücken. Ein Mann, der sich seiner geistigen Möglichkeiten noch gar nicht bewusst war, träumte, er entdecke in seinem Keller einen wunderbaren, fremdartigen, reich geschmückten Schatzkasten. Und oft erscheint in Träumen das Motiv des grossen Hauses, in dem noch unbekannte Räume voll kostbarer Dinge gefunden werden. Einer Frau, die nach langer Analyse zuletzt selbst Analytikerin wurde, träumte es schon viele Jahre zuvor, sie entdecke in einer unterirdischen Höhle eine Heilquelle, deren Fassung eine lange und geduldige Arbeit erfordere. Jemand, mit einer schriftstellerischen Arbeit beschäftigt, war in den Fehler verfallen, sich ironisch über einen ernsthaften Gegenstand zu äussern. Ihm träumte, eine grosse Künstlerin, eine Malerin mythischer Phantasien, sei gestorben, weil in zynischer Weise über ihre Bilder geschrieben worden sei. Dieser Traum liess den Schriftsteller gewahr werden, dass die Künstlerin in ihm stirbt, wenn sein Bewusstsein den Bildern des Unbewussten gegenüber eine unernste Haltung einnimmt.

Alle die genannten Traumbilder zeigen deutlich, wie das Mächtigere, das Überlegene und das Kostbare, im Unbewussten liegen kann und das Ich dabei das Empfangende ist. Sie lassen auch erkennen, wie das Ich eine richtige, bescheidene Einstellung braucht, damit es etwas von jenen Schätzen bekommt, und dass es den Willen aufbringen muss,

Anstrengungen und Opfer auf sich zu nehmen. Es ist wie in den Märchen, wo der Held dienen und sich unterordnen muss. Er hat alle möglichen Ansprüche zu opfern und oft mühselige und gefährliche Arbeiten zu verrichten, bis ihm die ersehnte Kostbarkeit zufällt. So könnte es vielleicht für den heutigen Künstler die geforderte Mühe sein, eine neue, der Epoche entsprechende Ausdrucksweise zu erarbeiten, die den Inhalten des Unbewussten gerecht wird. Es ist ein Ringen darum, das beinahe Undarstellbare sichtbar zu machen. Je ernster der Maler das innere Bild nimmt, desto grösser wird sein Wunsch nach bestmöglicher Gestaltung werden.

Als um die Jahrhundertwende die moderne Kunst sich von aller Tradition abwenden musste, lösten die Künstler sich auch von der traditionellen handwerklichen Technik. Das überlieferte Darstellenkönnen, erlernt mit grosser Arbeit durch minuziöse Ausbildung in figürlichem Zeichnen, Perspektive usw., war nicht an sich verwerflich. Es war eher der Missbrauch abzulehnen, den die naturalistische Kunst des 19. Jahrhunderts damit getrieben hat. All dieses ererbte Gut, dieses Wissen und Können aufzugeben, könnte fragwürdig erscheinen. Und doch ist es nicht zu übersehen, dass es das Ausdrucksmittel einer immer einseitiger, extravertiert gewordenen Kunst war – in geradezu naturwissenschaftlicher Weise zugespitzt –, um jede Einzelheit des Äussern zu erfassen. Die Gefahr dieser klassischen Technik liegt darin, dass damit dargestellte innere Gegenstände zu sehr auf die Seite des Stofflichen gezogen und dadurch verfälscht werden könnten. Andrerseits scheint es auch noch keine befriedigende Lösung darzustellen, sich mit den beschriebenen modernen Zufallsbildungen und Formlosigkeiten zu begnügen, wie sie etwa durch Gerinnung von Farben entstehen. Das wäre ungefähr, wie wenn man sich mit dem Finden einer originell gewachsenen Wurzel als Ausdruck des Unbewussten zufriedengäbe. Vermutlich sind solche Anregungen der Phantasie erst die Basis – etwas wie die *prima materia* –, aus der dann das Wertvolle in mühsamer Arbeit herausdestilliert werden muss.

Aus dem, was ich bis dahin zu schildern versuchte, geht hervor, dass heute die Kunst nicht mehr als eine bloss ästhetische Frage angesehen werden kann. Sie ist nicht ein Selbstzweck nach dem Motto *L'art pour l'art*, sondern muss wieder als eine Hilfe betrachtet werden, neuen, unbekannten, drängenden seelischen Inhalten Ausdruck zu verschaffen. Das Ich muss sich dabei als das Empfangende verhalten können, was eine religiöse Einstellung erfordert, Religion im Sinne von sorgfältiger Beobachtung und Berücksichtigung psychischer Faktoren. Während die alte religiöse Kunst Bilder allgemein sanktionierter, dogmatischer Vorstellungen brachte, steht der heutige Künstler mit seinen Erlebnissen allein, allen Irrtümern preisgegeben. Jung schrieb in *Psychologie und Religion*: «Ein Dogma ist immer das Resultat und die Frucht von vielen Geistern und vielen Jahrhunderten. Es ist gereinigt von allem Bizarren, von allem Unzulänglichen und Störenden der individuellen Erfahrung. Aber trotz alledem ist die individuelle Erfahrung gerade in ihrer Armseligkeit unmittelbares Leben, sie ist das warme, rote Blut, das heute pulsiert. Sie ist einem Wahrheitssucher überzeugender als die beste Tradition.»[7] Mit dieser Art individuellen Erlebens ist wieder etwas wie ein Urzustand hergestellt, da individuelle Visionen die innere Welt enthüllen. Es ist ein Neu-Anfang.

Jung hat sich vor allem als Arzt gesehen, aber es ist immer deutlicher geworden, dass er nicht nur einzelne Kranke heilte, sondern zum Arzt seines ganzen Zeitalters wurde. Indem er vielen Menschen dazu verhalf, eine Beziehung zur produktiven, führenden und ordnenden Seite der Seele zu bekommen, stellte er das Problem des psychischen Leidens in viel weitere Zusammenhänge. Dieses Leiden wurde dadurch weniger eine Krankheit als ein Abgeschnittensein vom Wesentlichen und von der eigenen Bestimmung. Diese Tat entreisst den heutigen Menschen der trostlosen und aussichtslosen Enge der materialistischen Weltanschauung und verschafft ihm die Möglichkeit, selbst die Tätigkeit jener schicksalshaften Macht zu erfahren, die seinem Leben einen eigenen Sinn verleiht.

In der Atmosphäre des Rationalismus kann das Psychische nicht leben; er ist wie ein Stein, der auf der Pflanze liegt, auf jenem eigenwilligen schöpferischen Keim, der sich aus der Seele entfalten möchte. Jung hat ihn von dieser Last befreit. Er hat jenen geistigen Trieb des Unbewussten nicht nur theoretisch beschrieben, sondern auch die Beispiele seiner Tätigkeit gezeigt und das eigene Leben durch ihn gestalten lassen.

Damit kann Jung wohl ein Leitbild sein für den heutigen Künstler, der einen Weg sucht zur Schatzkammer seiner Seele. Von jenem kostbaren Behältnis schrieb er das schöne und tröstliche Wort: «Ich glaube, dass kein wesentlicher Inhalt je verlorenging, weil seine Matrix immer in uns liegt, und er aus ihr aufs neue hervorgehen kann und hervorgehen wird, sobald man seiner bedarf.»[8]

Vortrag, gehalten an der C.G.-Jung-Gedenkfeier am 6. Juni 1970 in Zürich.

7 C. G. Jung, *Psychologie und Religion*, GW 11, § 88

8 C. G. Jung, *Briefe III*, Brief an Miguel Serrano vom 14. September, 1960. Olten & Freiburg im Breisgau: Walter-Verlag, 1973, S. 343.

PETER BIRKHÄUSER – A MODERN ARTIST WHO STRIKES A NEW PATH

Marie-Louise von Franz[1]

C. G. Jung has often pointed out that in the cultural sphere art frequently anticipates psychological changes before they come to the surface of collective awareness. Long before the First World War – in times which were still apparently peaceful – we saw a terrific breaking up of all the forms in our culture. This not only anticipated the coming catastrophe but also represented a turning-point in our general mental attitude – as Dr. Jung pointed out, a turning away from the outer objective world and an attempt to break all ties to it – in other words, the coming to an end of the purely extraverted attitude which has dominated art since the Renaissance.[2]

But where will we go from here? Since we cannot remain forever in that iconoclastic mood, many modern artists are seeking for new and different forms. Peter Birkhäuser of Basel is one of these. His unusual talent led him to find modes of expression which drew Dr. Jung's attention and won his appreciation; for Birkhäuser's turning away from outer objects had a different character from that of most non-objective modern painters. In contrast to the abstract painters and many of the surrealists, and perhaps under the influence of his teacher Niklaus Stoecklin, he did at first paint outer objects, but they increasingly acquired an uncanny, demonic or 'dead' quality. Motifs, such as appeared in his still life of some mandragora-like leguminous roots or his painting of a dead leaf with a demonic fly sitting on it, haunted him, until – in the crisis of middle life, together with the wearing out of the superior function (which in his case is introverted sensation) – a completely new 'form' broke through. Then he began to paint the 'inner world', not the *massa confusa* of the surrealists or tachists but the inner archetypal images. And, being a true artist, he seems to me to have avoided the pitfall of painting merely his own personal, unconscious

1 This essay by Marie-Louise von Franz was published in *Spring, Contributions to Jungian Thought*, New York 1964.

2 Aniela Jaffé, "Symbolism in the Visual Arts", in: *C. G. Jung, Man and His Symbols,* New York 1968.

problems and to have succeeded in giving expression to deeper, more generally valid 'events' in the collective unconscious.

Jung once said, in a London seminar that: "[...] man's relation to the collective unconscious has always been regulated. There is a characteristic form by which the archetypal images are expressed. For *the collective unconscious is a function that always operates and man has to keep in touch with it.* His psychical and spiritual health depends upon the co-operation of the impersonal images. Therefore, man has always had his religions."[3]

Today, as we said to begin with, the old forms of our culture have broken down, but our need to relate to the living inner reality of the archetypal images remains and their pressure is felt by us all.

Originally art was not dissociated from religion as it is with us. Consider the Naskapi Indians for example, a most primitive group of hunters living on the Labrador peninsula, so primitive that they have no religion, no social, tribal organization, no leaders, no rites, no medicine men, and also no artists – in our sense of the term.[4] But if asked what they believe, they reply that man has Mistap'eo – the 'Great Man' – dwelling in his heart and that Mistap'eo sends guiding dreams to everybody. If these are attended to, the dreamer gets more dreams and better ones. The only 'religious' obligation they recognize is to pay attention to their dreams and 'test them out'; also, *to try to represent relevant dream motifs graphically,* for that too, they say, pleases Mistap'eo. So they paint these motifs on their ladles, tents, trays, shotpouches, and the like. Here we still have an unusual example of the 'togetherness' of religion, art, and an individual, personal relationship to the unconscious. The Naskapi's pictures are not just art, they have a religious function and they are a part of the attention owed to Mistap'eo, the 'Great Man in the Heart'.

I read in a newspaper recently of a Macedonian peasant healer who has fallen back into this primitive kind of original ritual: he heals people (mostly those whose diseases are psychogenic) in the following way: the patient must sit in front of a whitewashed wall with the healer standing behind him; then suddenly the healer is mediumistically inspired and draws what he 'sees' on the wall in red lines. The sight of this picture heals the patient. Obviously, he is cured because he can now see consciously before him what was previously

3 C. G. Jung, "On the Theory and Practice of Analytical Psychology", in: *The Symbolic Life*, CW 18, § 369. My italics.

4 Frank G. Speck, *Naskapi: The Savage Hunters of the Labrador Peninsula*. University Oklahoma Press, 1935.

haunting him from behind. When I once told Dr. Jung that his discoveries and way of relating to the unconscious seemed to me more like the most primitive stone age forms of religion than anything more recent, he laughed and said: "Yes, and it is not to our discredit!" He meant that by directly relating to the archetypal images we really return to the most natural, basic *anthropos* within us. It seems to me that the artist also has to return to these fundamental original forms, in order to paint in a healing way figures which would otherwise haunt us from behind our backs.

The break-through into awareness of another transcendental unitary universe, beyond our visible reality, has been painted by Peter Birkhäuser in "The Fourth Dimension" (plate 7) – a painting which is also reproduced in "Flying Saucers, A Modern Myth of Things Seen in the Skies", and there commented on by Dr. Jung at some length.[5] It represents the becoming visible of another dimension which cuts across our reality (represented by the red town) and which is animated by a divine spirit whose features are half human and half animal. This new dimension is 'spotted' in a strange way with round dots, like knots or focal points within the flowing expansion of the strange divine being. One could call this a picture of the *unus mundus* and its dynamic concentrations (that is, the archetypes), especially as they manifest themselves in synchronistic events.[6]

In the pictures discussed here we encounter some of the dynamic nodal points which appeared in "The Fourth Dimension", powers which seem to exert a special pressure upon us at the present time. Plate 8 is called "Imprisoned Creative Power" by the artist, but has also been aptly named "The Earthquake Animal". One certainly realizes with horror (and so evidently does the little fleeing man on the right at the bottom) that if this Behemoth, with its starry golden eye, moves only a little, the whole mountain which contains him will collapse and explode into flames. It is an earthquake from within that we all fear, the danger that a new divine revelation from the unconscious, failing to find its way through into consciousness, might destroy it instead. If our civilization should be destroyed by the atom bomb, it will – at bottom – be fundamentally because this animal has not been able to come forth and free itself. Its golden eye stares out of the picture with the look that we see in a bird's eye, which does not focus immediately ahead but is constructed to look at things from afar. This shows that the animal carries within itself the germ of a new consciousness,

5 C. G. Jung, "Flying Saucers, A Modern Myth of Things Seen in the Skies", in: *Civilisation in Transition*, CW 10, § 736-747.

6 C. G. Jung, *Mysterium Coniunctionis*, CW 14, § 660 f.

but a remote and objective consciousness, far removed from everyday human concerns. The animal is turned toward the left of the picture; it is not oriented in the direction generally identified with consciousness, and that is another reason why it is 'imprisoned'. It just stands there under the terrific weight of molten boulders and one has no idea what it will do. Its features are those of a paleontological saurian, a very early species of animal life. Such saurian motifs always point – as Dr. Jung once told me – to creative power, because "In those times", he said jokingly, "God just revelled in shapes and colours, He attempted all sorts of new forms: reptiles which could fly like birds, enormous fleshy monsters with long necks and tiny heads, queer new constructions like feathers and all kinds of fantastic beings. But then He felt that there should be something on top (here Dr. Jung pointed to where the head is), that something should grow there. So the Creator tried first with warts and funny little horns, but that didn't work. At last, quite suddenly, He knew: what was needed was more brain inside! After that He invented the higher mammals, and the saurians just lay down and died – out of sheer despair about their own stupidity!" That is why one so often finds saurian motifs in the dreams of creative artists.

The man who is leaving his car in a panic (at the bottom of plate 8) is not only small but colourless as a diagram – all the energy and life is stored up in the fiery animal and its mountain cover. This shows the extent of the disproportion in our lives: consciously things are technical, rational, colourless and schematic, but the unconscious powers of creative fantasy, because they no longer find an outlet, have become destructive. This animal is very like some medieval pictures of Behemoth and Leviathan and thus it may also be thought of as representing the dark side of the Creator – that side of the godhead which we must now recognize and relate to, if we can hope to avoid being destroyed by it.

In the next picture, called "Fire Gives Birth" (plate 9), the whole situation has changed. The flames, which are only just issuing from their mountain-prison in plate 8, have burst forth in a fiery stream and are taking form as a cluster of different shapes, stems, leaves, flowers, a caterpillar, and at the very tip a barely discernible satyr-like human head. The creative spirit of nature, miraculous and incomprehensible, is vomiting forth all these forms of life and we too are produced by that spirit, tossed into space by a great power with unknown intentions: this is a representation of how modern man feels when he loses the strongholds of tradition.

The motif of the flower, which appears first in this picture, has often been repeated in Birkhäuser's paintings; eyes like flowers, flowery garments and the like seem to express the miracle of mathematical form which is realized in the growth of a living being. Flowers are the innocent thoughts of the Creator. "The early manifestations of 'God's world', Jung said, began with the realm of plants, as a kind of direct communication from it. It was as though one were peering over the shoulder of the Creator, who, thinking Himself unobserved, was making toys and decorations. Man and the proper animals, on the other hand, were bits of God that had become independent. That was why they could move about on their own and choose their abodes. Plants were bound for good or ill to their places. They expressed not only beauty, but also the thoughts of God's world, with no intent of their own and without deviation."[7]

These wondrous formations of the creative spirit are represented in our picture, and man too is amongst them; for, though unfortunately he is infinitely more complicated and problematic, the goal of all this fiery birth process seems to be man. That is, man is its goal in the sense that, as Meister Eckhart said, "All cereal means wheat, all treasure nature means gold, all generation means man."[8] Human consciousness is the goal of evolution (on this earth at least) and we do not know what the divine powers will still produce through us.

The next picture Birkhäuser painted was of a beautiful black youth with four arms riding on a boar-like, hairy white horse, a magical flower growing from his outstretched hand ("Puer Aeternus", plate 11). When the artist showed him these three pictures, "Imprisoned Creative Power", "Fire Gives Birth" and "Puer Aeternus" Dr. Jung's comment about the first was: "The animal which is imprisoned in the mountain is a content of the unconscious exerting a strong pressure; it is something in the soul, perhaps also in the body, which could provoke an explosion. Inadequate emotional outbursts often characterize such a situation." And of the second he said: "Now the content is breaking out from the hot waves of libido [at the right], one could also say from the waves of emotion and excited feeling. Such wave-like curves often appear in the pictures of feeling types. It is creative energy – these forms remind one of ectoplasm. This is what Goethe meant by 'The creation! Image of all creatures!' *(Faust).* The man [whose satyr-like head appears] has something demonic about him, the beginning of devilish horror." Then Jung added, "Creation is completely demonic, wonderful – an awe-inspiring and terrible secret. If one considers how the caterpillar spins its cocoon and how the chrysalis already takes the shape of the future butterfly even while the caterpillar is dissolved into milky fluid [...] We always assume that *we* are responsible for

7 C. G. Jung, *Memories, Dreams, Reflections*, ed. by Aniela Jaffé, p. 67.

8 Meister Eckhart, *Sermons and Collations* XXIX, translated by C. de B. Evans, Vol. I, p. 80.

attaching the stalks to the cherries – whereas in reality we are only instrumental!" "In the third picture ("Puer Aeternus"), he pointed out: "the dark beast has been liberated and now it's riding through the distant heavens in the form of a white boar-like horse. This is the white horse Pegasus, carrying Aquarius, or the *puer aeternus, albus et ater.* The god reveals himself to everyone. That is what people can't understand. I can't tell you here all the things associated with this picture of the *puer.* It's connected with the continuing process of god becoming man."

Before Birkhäuser painted these pictures, when he first began to allow the collective unconscious to express itself through him, his pictures showed many very dark and uncanny motifs: a split man ("The World's Wound", plate 2), a hunchbacked boy coming up from the sewers but carrying a lamp (plate 5), a green horse-faced space-demon seizing a lonely airplane, a four-eyed face spitting lightning at a terrified man who turns away in despair, and many others, a pandemonium of weird and fearful apparitions that remind one of Hieronymus Bosch. Such a first welling up of the unconscious often has a frightening and dark aspect. In the time of transition, when the artist began to allow inner contents to break into the world of outer reality, he also painted an old witch-like woman with the face of a cat, a picture which Dr. Jung owned and kept in his study (plate 3). Other present-day artists have expressed this destruction of outer reality by means of distorted, shattered and ugly forms, and Birkhäuser, who as a sensation type has a high sensitivity to beautiful form, suffered greatly from this need to represent the darkness. In contrast to many other modern painters, however, he did not discard form completely but tried to express even the most dark, uncanny and destructive powers in carefully formed shapes. This gives his pictures their unique character. Many artists who paint the inner fantasy world try to express the difference between it and outer reality by giving it somewhat blurred shapes, or by blending motifs as if several photographs were being taken over each other (Chagall). But Birkhäuser chose another way, he gave to his figures forms with a subtle-body quality or a ghost-like transparency. This – and the dark colours he often uses for his background – lends many of his paintings a 'nocturnal' feeling quality which conveys the reality of the unconscious. An analysand of mine, of a sensation type, who could never fully believe in the reality of the unconscious, was quite overwhelmed when he saw Birkhäuser's paintings and said: "Now for the first time I can *see* those powers which I feared and yet tried to believe did not exist. Now at last they are real to me."

The overwhelmingly threatening and dangerous aspect of the unconscious is represented in many of Birkhäuser's earlier paintings, and some of its gruesome darkness persists in the picture he calls "The Outcast" (plate 10), a strange demon, walking over and away from an industrial town. The town is all colourless and grey again, presenting that unnatural, dead, 'technical', rational world of ours, from which the powers of creative imagination and the spirit of nature are cast out. The face of the banished ghost is divided in the middle by a line of shadows. He is probably the *Mercurius duplex* of the alchemists, that divine spirit in matter, who is "good with the good and bad with the bad". We ourselves are split and therefore even the divine spirit in matter cannot express himself in his wholeness but has to assume a dual character – for one could say: "The tortured tortures and the split splits!" His feet are stiff, clumsy, heavy and unnatural, and one feels that he could trample down things inadvertently, just as the earthquake animal (plate 8) also could be unintentionally destructive. In another picture Birkhäuser painted an irascible dwarf with leaden feet. Lead is the metal of Saturn, a symbol of the 'depressing' quality of the unconscious, that depression which is also the *prima materia* of all creativeness. This gives to the Outcast a double aspect of destroyer and savior, and the rainbow colours of the 'ectoplasmic-flag' which he drags behind him suggest this saving aspect too. When the lead is cooked in the alchemistic process, there is a stage directly after the *nigredo* when "all colours appear" and the old masters say that this is the moment when the soul (of matter) becomes manifest.[9] The soul is a 'vapor' and that is probably why the 'flag' or fiery comet's tail in our picture is so like ectoplasm: it is soul stuff, so to speak. Thus the Outcast is very much like Mercurius – or the 'spirit in matter' of the alchemists – who has been banished by our materialistic age and has taken all life and colour with him. But there is a further great danger represented in this picture: Mercurius is walking to the left (like the Behemoth in plate 8); he moves toward the unconscious as if on the way to disappear into it, and the flag he drags behind him looks dangerously like some device to set fire to the town below and behind him. As we are all immediately in danger of being killed by fire and radioactivity – especially in our big industrial towns – this fiery flag has a most timely and terrifying aspect. Will the divine spirit in nature – and in our unconscious – that power which our rationalism and commercialism have raped and violated, kill us in this way before leaving us? Will it trample down our whole world and then disappear into the unknown from whence it came? But

9 C. G. Jung, *Mysterium Coniunctionis*, CW 14, § 391 f.

there are also hopeful and reconciling elements in the picture: the demon has white hair like the Ancient of Days – there is apparently some age-old and great wisdom in him – and the many-coloured fiery flag is reminiscent of the rainbow, which God created to remind Himself that He promised never to exterminate mankind again as He tried to do in the flood. So this demonic godhead still carries that reminder, the reconciling symbol, and it hovers like a simultaneous danger and protection over our heads.

The face of the Outcast is blue and bluish green in colour, suggesting that he originated in the depths of water and in the world of vegetation, two things which, now especially, we constantly destroy and contaminate to our own detriment. The claws and the reddish hairy coat point to the animal nature of this spirit. Taken together with his Mercurius aspect, these qualities indicate that he unites the mineral, vegetable, and animal kingdoms within himself.

But claws and a furry coat are not the only weird features of the Outcast; he also has a split face, as was mentioned above, and a humpback. A man with this deformity – as is well known – is often considered lucky. In Italy, for instance, people crowd round a hunchback because it brings luck to touch his hump. Yet this motif indicates that the Spirit is distorted and a cripple. He is split like a split and shadowy man painted earlier by Birkhäuser (plate 2). The hunchback also appeared in another early painting as a pale red-haired boy climbing up a ladder out of a sewer (plate 5). This crippled boy represented the Outcast in human shape as a distorted, unhappy, unhealthy, proletarian boy, who inspired one simultaneously with pity and awe. Dr. Jung once said, in an interview which he gave to a city-planner, that what modern man most needs is a bit of land of his own, a little house or garden to himself, where he can live out his imaginings and his creative fantasies. (This is the reason for the great success of the allotment movement).[10] If one piles up men in prefabricated flats, in collective cement boxes, they consciously or unconsciously miss a vital element of life and then blame capitalism or something else for this condition. For if man's most basic instincts can no longer live he becomes destructive. In the right eye of the Outcast (when the other is covered) one sees a murderous stare of madness, while the left eye is full of suffering and looks upward for help from above. This seems to me to truly express the condition of that part of the psyche which collectivity has cast out from life today: it is not yet decided whether it will turn into sheer destructiveness or whether its suffering will constellate a

10 In the 19th century the idea came up of renting small spots in the waste areas around towns to people who had no land of their own for use as gardens. Such gardens exist all over Europe now and are very popular.

helpful change in our collective attitude. The duality and suspense of this situation seems to me mirrored in the picture.

The "Twin Fish" (plate 12) is a later painting and shows an increase of colour and light. The shimmer of the water breaks up its shining surface and a blue eye (a mirror image of the eye of the viewer?) looks out of the watery depths. It is the eye which looks at us from the depths of our own psyche, and which gives us the strange feeling that we are 'watched' by a suprapersonal power in whatever we do. It expresses the larger view that St. Paul foretold when he said, "Now I know in part; but then shall I know even as I am known". (I Cor. 13,12) If we want to gain objective knowledge of ourselves, insight which is not born from subjective thoughts about our own ego, we must try to find out how this other eye in the depths of our soul sees us, for in this sense we are 'known' before we 'shall know'.

Fishes' eyes and sparks are often treated as one theme in alchemy, which is why Gerhardus Dorn's remarks about sparks may be understood as applying to the famous alchemical motif of the fish's eyes.[11] He says: "Thus little by little he [the adept] will come to see with his mental eyes a number of sparks shining day by day and more and more and growing into such a great light that thereafter all things needful to him will be known."[12]

Commenting on Dorn's statement, Dr. Jung goes on to explain: "This light is the *lumen naturae* which illuminates consciousness and the *scintillae* are germinal luminosities shining forth from the darkness of the unconscious."

In plate 12 the blue eye of the waters stands in contrast to the red eye of the fish, which is at the centre of a flower-like shape. This red eye of the fish is in a way rather like that of the earthquake animal: both have the form of mandalas, but it is as if the centre which at first only expressed itself in an even ordered form, has now begun to 'see' what is in the waters – and to see with great passion (red). This eye might well represent the 'new sight' which the fourth function brings to consciousness. Its awakening gives insight into hitherto unknown areas of life. In Birkhäuser's type it would be the eye of intuition which enables him to see all these great powers of the collective unconscious.

The fish is semi-transparent, a fact which gives it a 'spiritual' quality and the figures of two beautiful young men embracing each other are visible inside its body.[13] Who are these youths who share the transparent subtle-body quality and the magical beauty of the fish?

11 C. G. Jung, "On the Nature of the Psyche", in: *The Structure and Dynamics of the Psyche*, CW 8, § 394.
12 C. G. Jung, "On the Nature of the Psyche", in: *The Structure and Dynamics of the Psyche*, CW 8, § 389.
13 *Diaphanitas*, or diaphanousness, was understood by the alchemists as implying a spiritual nature.

The fish motif combined with various others often appears in mythologies familiar to us. Not only is Christ represented as a fish but in *Aion* Dr. Jung mentions many examples of fishermen and fish who came up from the depths of the unconscious to save mankind. The great Babylonian wisdom teacher, Oannes was also thought to have come up from the sea in the shape of a fish and therefore his priests wore fish skin garments. Vishnu saved the holy scriptures in India by diving down in the shape of a fish to save the Vedas from the floods. So it is not surprising that this fish should carry within it a saviour figure, in the shape of a youth. One of Birkhäuser's earlier pictures, which I mentioned above (plate 11), was of this same youth riding on a wild, white horse like a boar with a magic flower growing from his outstretched hand. The *puer aeternus,* the new saving content coming from the unconscious, brings into the world the 'sacred spring' of which Virgil had dreamed long before. This new saving content, seen from the human angle, would represent a renewed possibility of religious inner experience. But here there are *two* youths, twin-friends, in the fish and one is tempted to think of that famous verse in the *Upanishads*:

> "Behold upon the selfsame tree,
> Two birds, fast-bound companions sit.
> This one enjoys the ripened fruit,
> The other looks, but does not eat."[14]

Those two represent the basic opposites in our psyche, and also the movements towards extraversion (eating was interpreted in India as 'eating the world') and introversion. In our part of the world, the opposites are in much greater opposition or even in strife. Horus and Set in Egypt, and Christ and the Satanael with us, have become hostile brothers, the warring principles of good and evil. The light brother, Christ, rejected his shadow, which therefore became his opponent, even his enemy. This split has now reached our whole civilization where the opposites fight, stiffening in ever growing bitterness against each other. Nevertheless they are brothers, and once they came out of the same depths of the unconscious psyche. An old Bogomil apocryphal manuscript even describes these opposites as fishes, yoked together like oxen, who plough the surface of the waters. Jung says: "The comparison of the fishes with a yoke of oxen ploughing merits special attention. Oxen

14 C. G. Jung, *Symbols of Transformation,* CW 5, § 296 and Shvetâshvatara Upanishad, IV,6.

stand for the motive powers of the plough. In the same way the fishes represent the driving forces of the coming world of consciousness [...] The ploughing or mastering of the earth is undertaken 'at the command of the Father'. Thus God not only foresaw the enantiodromia that began in the year 1000, but also intended it. The Platonic month of the Fishes is ruled by two principles. The fishes in this context are parallel, like the oxen, and point to the same goal, although one is Christ and the other is the Antichrist."[15]

Although we have only one fish in our picture, its inner duality is represented by the two youths. The opposites are here not only renewed but are even reunited in loving embrace and the fish carries them *downwards* into the water regions and to *the left.* It is probably only because of this that they can unite. If the fish goes even further and deeper, the two may actually dissolve and become *one* divine figure again. When their becoming one has been achieved, the fish may return upwards and give birth to a new saving symbol: the figure of a saviour or of united twin-brothers in complete harmony, such as the Ashvins in India, or Castor and Pollux, the great helpers in distress at sea.[16] As Dr. Jung pointed out in *Aion,* the fish symbol often has such a dual and hermaphroditic aspect for it is a *complexio oppositorum,* and it is seen in a biblical context also in the 'miraculous food', the eucharistic food of the *teleioi*."[17]

"Twin Fish" is not Birkhäuser's last painting; he has gone further since and I continue to be surprised at the new turns his motifs and style take. He does not stand still but, like so many artists, is ever urged to go further and further by his creative demon, to try out new ways again and again. The creative urge is so strong in him that he has to save all his strength to satisfy its demands; and therefore he lives a rather introverted and retired life with his family in Binningen near Basel. He has no time for such stunt-displays as those of Salvador Dalí, but he nevertheless reaches people. Once when a printing firm was reproducing one of his pictures a young girl who worked there saw the proof and rang him up to say she was so impressed that she would like to see more of his pictures. So she came with a whole group of young people. They were delighted and showed a great deal of understanding of the paintings. This seems to show that already the younger generation is naturally approaching closer to these inner facts which Jung, as a lonely pioneer, discovered far ahead of his time.

15 C. G. Jung, *Aion,* CW 9/II, § 231.

16 C. G. Jung, *Symbols of Transformation,* CW 5, § 296.

17 C. G. Jung, *Aion,* CW 9/II, § 237. The *teleioi* were the perfect ones, those who reached completeness in a specific Gnostic sense, enlightened gnosis of God.

The youngsters' only disappointment was that Birkhäuser did not look like the bearded Bohemian they had expected! But anyone who knows him well can see the hidden fire within him, which he covers with a quiet and introverted manner. A young man who once visited him said: "When I left that little garden studio, I looked back at it full of wonder that such a little hut should contain such precious and overwhelming powers."

PETER BIRKHÄUSER – EIN MODERNER KÜNSTLER AUF NEUEM WEG

Marie-Louise von Franz[1]

C. G. Jung hat öfter bemerkt, dass die Wandlungsprozesse der Psyche im kulturellen Sektor – insbesondere in den Künsten – zutage treten, bevor sie an die Oberfläche des kollektiven Bewusstseins gelangen. Lange vor dem Ersten Weltkrieg, als die Zeiten scheinbar noch friedlich waren, kam es zu einer gewaltigen Zersplitterung der Formen. Dieses Phänomen nahm nicht nur die kommende Katastrophe vorweg, sondern markierte einen Wendepunkt in der allgemeinen geistigen Einstellung. Jung beschrieb diesen Umschlag als Abkehr von der äusseren Welt der Gegenstände und als Versuch, die Bindungen zur Objektwelt zu lösen – mit anderen Worten: Er erkannte in der Fragmentierung der Formen das Ende der rein extravertierten Haltung, die die Kunst seit der Renaissance dominiert hatte.[2]

Aber wie geht es jetzt weiter? Schliesslich können wir nicht ewig in einer ikonoklastischen Stimmung verharren. Viele moderne Künstler sind auf der Suche nach einer neuen und anderen Formsprache – Peter Birkhäuser aus Basel ist einer von ihnen. Seine aussergewöhnliche Begabung führte ihn zu Ausdrucksformen, die auch Jungs Aufmerksamkeit erregten und seine Zustimmung fanden. Denn Birkhäusers Abkehr vom äusseren Gegenstand hatte im Vergleich zur Mehrzahl abstrakt arbeitender Maler einen völlig anderen Charakter. Im Gegensatz zu seinen ungegenständlich malenden Kollegen und vielen figürlich arbeitenden Surrealisten malte Birkhäuser (möglicherweise unter dem Einfluss seines Lehrers Niklaus Stoecklin) zunächst äussere Dinge, die aber zunehmend eine unheimliche, dämonische oder gar «tote» Qualität aufwiesen. Motive, wie sie in seinen frühen Stillleben erscheinen, etwa alraunenartig wuchernde Wurzeln von Hülsenfrüchten oder ein totes Blatt mit einer dämonischen Fliege, verfolgten ihn. In der Krise der Lebensmitte brach – parallel zur Abnutzung der übergeordneten Funktion (die in seinem Fall

1 Dieser Essay wurde erstmals veröffentlicht in: *Spring. Contributions to Jungian Thought*, New York 1964.

2 Vgl.: Aniela Jaffé, «Bildende Kunst als Symbol», in: C. G. Jung, *Der Mensch und seine Symbole*. Zürich, Düsseldorf: Walter, [16]2003, S. 187, 199.

die introvertierte Empfindung ist) – schliesslich eine völlig neue «Form» durch. Von da an begann er, die innere Welt zu malen: nicht die *massa confusa* der Surrealisten oder Tachisten, sondern innere archetypische Bilder. Als wahrer Künstler hat er es vermieden, seine eigenen, persönlichen unbewussten Probleme zu malen; vielmehr ist es ihm in seinen Gemälden gelungen, tiefere, allgemein gültige Ereignisse im kollektiven Unbewussten darzustellen.

Jung äusserte einmal in einem Londoner Seminar, dass «... die Beziehung des Menschen zum kollektiven Unbewussten immer in Normen gefasst [war]; es gibt eine charakteristische Form, in der die archetypischen Bilder ausgedrückt werden. Denn *das kollektive Unbewusste ist eine Funktion, die immer am Werk ist, und der Mensch muss die Fühlung mit ihr behalten*. Seine psychische und geistige Gesundheit hängt von der Mitarbeit der unpersönlichen Bilder ab. Daher hatte der Mensch stets seine Religionen.»[3] Heute sind, wie gesagt, die alten Formen unserer Kultur zerbrochen – aber das Bedürfnis, mit der lebendigen inneren Realität der archetypischen Bilder in Beziehung zu treten, besteht weiter. Dieser «Druck» ist für uns alle fühlbar.

Ursprünglich war die Kunst nicht von der Religion getrennt, wie es in unserer Zeit der Fall ist. Denken Sie zum Beispiel an die Naskapi-Indianer, eine Gruppe von Jägern, die auf der Labrador-Halbinsel leben. Dieses indigene Volk ist so ursprünglich organisiert, dass es ohne Religion und ohne soziale Stammesstruktur auskommt. Sie haben keine Anführer, keine Riten, keine Medizinmänner und auch keine Künstler in unserem Sinn.[4] Fragt man die Naskapi, an was sie glauben, erwidern sie, dass Mistap'eo, der «Grosse Mann», in den Herzen der Menschen wohnt und jedem von ihnen wegweisende Träume schickt. Die einzige religiöse Verpflichtung, die sie anerkennen, besteht darin, ihren Träumen Beachtung zu schenken und sie «auszuprobieren». Ausserdem versuchen sie, wichtige Traummotive grafisch darzustellen, denn auch das, so sagen sie, gefällt Mistap'eo. Also malen sie diese Motive auf ihre Schöpfkellen, Zelte, Tabletts, Schnapsgläser und dergleichen. Wir haben hier noch ein ungewöhnliches Beispiel für die Zusammengehörigkeit von Religion, Kunst und einer individuellen, persönlichen Beziehung zum Unbewussten. Die Bilder der Nas-

3 C. G. Jung: «Über die Grundlagen der Analytischen Psychologie», in: *Das symbolische Leben*, Gesammelte Werke (GW) 18/1, § 369. Hervorhebung: M. L. von Franz.

4 Vgl. dazu: Frank G. Speck, *Naskapi. The Savage Hunters of the Labrador Peninsula.* University Oklahoma Press, 1935.

kapi sind nicht nur Kunst, sie haben zugleich eine religiöse Funktion und sind Teil der Hingabe an Mistap'eo, den «Grossen Mann im Herzen».

Neulich las ich von einem mazedonischen Volksheiler in der Zeitung, der in den primitiven Modus des ursprünglichen Rituals zurückfiel. Dieser Mann heilt Menschen (meist solche, deren Krankheiten psychischer Herkunft sind) auf folgende Weise: Der Patient muss vor einer weiss getünchten Wand sitzen und der Heiler steht hinter ihm. Er empfängt eine mediumistische Inspiration und zeichnet in roten Strichen an die Wand, was er vor seinem inneren Auge sieht. Der Anblick dieses Bildes heilt. Der Patient ist wieder gesund, denn er sieht jetzt bewusst, was ihn zuvor «von hinten» verfolgt hatte. Als ich Dr. Jung einmal gestand, dass mir seine Entdeckungen und seine Methode, sich auf das Unbewussten zu beziehen, wie eine primitive, steinzeitliche Form von Religion vorkam und nicht unserer modernen Zeit entsprungen, lachte er: «Ja, und das ist nicht zu unserem Schaden!» Jung ist der Auffassung, dass wir durch unmittelbaren Bezug auf archetypische Bilder zum natürlichen *anthropos* in uns zurückkehren. Ich denke, dass auch der Künstler zu jenen universellen Urformen zurückfinden muss, um Dinge zu malen, die uns hinter unserem Rücken verfolgen, und damit heilend zu wirken.

Den Durchbruch in das Bewusstwerden eines anderen, transzendentalen Universums jenseits unserer sichtbaren Realität hat Peter Birkhäuser in seinem Werk «Die vierte Dimension» (Abb. 7) dargestellt – ein Gemälde, das auch in Jungs Essay «Ein moderner Mythus. Von Dingen, die am Himmel gesehen werden» abgebildet und ausführlich kommentiert ist.[5] Es zeigt das Sichtbarwerden einer anderen Dimension, die unsere Realität (dargestellt in der roten Stadt) geheimnisvoll durchdringt und die von einem göttlichen Geist belebt wird, dessen Züge halb menschlich, halb tierisch sind. Diese neue Dimension ist durch eigenartige runde Punkte angedeutet, die wie Knoten oder Brennpunkte innerhalb der fliessenden Ausdehnung des seltsamen göttlichen Wesens wirken. Man könnte dieses Gemälde als Bild des *unus mundus* in seinen dynamischen Verdichtungen (d. h. den Archetypen) verstehen, etwa wenn diese sich in Form von synchronistischen Ereignissen äussern.[6]

Diesen Verdichtungen oder dynamischen Knotenpunkten, die im Werk «Die vierte Dimension» auftauchen und besonderen Druck auf uns und unsere Zeit ausüben, begeg-

5 C. G. Jung, «Ein moderner Mythus. Von Dingen, die am Himmel gesehen werden», in: *Zivilisation im Übergang*, GW 10, § 736-747.

6 Zur Idee des *unus mundus* vgl. C. G. Jung, *Mysterium Coniunctionis,* in: GW 14/2, § 325 f.

nen wir auch in anderen Bildern Birkhäusers. Zum Beispiel in dem Gemälde, das der Künstler «Tier im Berg» nannte (Abb. 8), das aber auch den treffenden Titel «Erdbebentier» trägt. Wie dem fliehenden kleinen Mann rechts unten am Bildrand wird auch uns Betrachtern mit Schrecken klar: Wenn das eingesperrte Behemoth-Ungeheuer mit seinem goldenen Sternenauge sich nur ein klein wenig bewegen sollte, wird der ganze Berg einstürzen und in Flammen aufgehen. Ein solches Erdbeben von innen fürchten wir insgeheim alle. Die Gefahr besteht, dass eine neue göttliche Offenbarung aus dem Unbewussten das Bewusstsein zerstört, wenn es ihr nicht gelingt, zu ihm durchzudringen.

Sollte die Möglichkeit der Auslöschung unserer Zivilisation durch die nukleare Bedrohung tatsächlich eintreten, läge die Ursache für diese Katastrophe darin, dass jenes Tier nicht aus seinem Berg hervorkommen, sich nicht befreien konnte. Der starre Blick, mit dem es uns anschaut, erinnert an ein Vogelauge, das nicht unmittelbar nach vorne blickt, sondern die Dinge aus der Ferne betrachtet. Am weitschauenden goldenen Auge des «Tiers im Berg» wird deutlich, dass es den Keim eines neuen Bewusstseins in sich trägt – aber es ist ein fernes und objektives Bewusstsein, das weit von den alltäglichen Sorgen der Menschen entfernt ist. Das Tier wendet sich zur linken Bildseite; es ist also nicht in die Richtung orientiert, die man gemeinhin mit dem Bewusstsein identifiziert – ein weiterer Grund, warum es gefangen sein könnte. Es steht einfach da unter dem gewaltigen Gewicht der geschmolzenen Gesteinsmassen und niemand weiss, was als nächstes geschehen wird. Sein Aussehen erinnert an einen Dinosaurier, eine sehr frühzeitliche Spezies.

Das Motiv des Sauriers im Allgemeinen deutet, wie Dr. Jung es einmal formulierte, auf schöpferische Schaffenskraft, denn «damals», so Jung scherzhaft, «schwelgte Gott geradezu in Formen und Farben, er probierte alle möglichen Dinge aus, schuf Reptilien, die wie Vögel fliegen konnten oder riesige fleischerne Ungeheuer mit langen Hälsen und winzigen Köpfen, eigenartige neue Konstruktionen wie Federn – alle möglichen phantastischen Geschöpfe bevölkerten in jenen Urzeiten die Erde. Aber dann hatte Gott das Gefühl, dass *oben* etwas sein sollte (hier zeigte Dr. Jung auf die Stelle, wo der Kopf ist), dass dort etwas entstehen sollte. Also versuchte Gott es zuerst mit Warzen und lustigen kleinen Hörnern, aber das funktionierte nicht. Endlich, urplötzlich, wusste er: Es muss mehr Gehirn hinein! Daraufhin erfand Gott die höheren Säugetiere. Die Dinosaurier legten sich einfach nieder und starben, aus schierer Verzweiflung über ihre eigene Dummheit.» Und so findet man in den Träumen von schöpferisch tätigen Künstlern das eigentümliche Motiv des Sauriers recht häufig.

Der Mann, der in Panik sein Auto verlässt, ist nicht nur winzig klein, sondern auch farblos wie in einer Schemazeichnung: alle Energie und Lebenskraft sind in dem feurigen Tier und dem umgebenden Berg versammelt. Darin zeigt sich das ganze Ausmass des Missverhältnisses, in dem Bewusstsein und Unbewusstes in unserem Leben zueinander stehen. Im Bewusstsein sind die Dinge technisch, rational, farblos und schematisch, im Unbewussten wiederum sind die Kräfte der schöpferischen Phantasie vollkommen destruktiv geworden – eben weil sie kein Ventil mehr finden. Das Tier in Birkhäusers Gemälde erinnert sehr an mittelalterliche Abbildungen von Behemoth und Leviathan und kann daher auch als Sinnbild für den dunklen Aspekt des Schöpfers betrachtet werden – jene Seite der Gottheit, die wir endlich anerkennen sollten und zu der wir in Beziehung treten müssen, wenn wir nicht von ihr vernichtet werden wollen.

Im nächsten Bild «Feuergeburt» (Abb. 9) hat sich die Situation grundlegend gewandelt. Die Flammen, die im «Tier im Berg» an einzelnen Stellen aus ihrem steinernen Gefängnis dringen, brechen nun in einem feurigen Strom hervor und treten als Bündel multipler Formen in Erscheinung: als Stängel, Blätter und Blüten, aber auch als Raupe und schliesslich sogar als ein im Formengewirr kaum erkennbarer satyrartiger Menschenkopf. Der schöpferische Geist der Natur spuckt, wundersam und unbegreiflich, all diese Gestalten aus. Auch wir werden von diesem Geist hervorgebracht, werden von einer grossen Macht mit unbekannten Absichten in den Weltenraum geworfen: Das Gemälde «Feuergeburt» stellt dar, was der moderne Mensch fühlt, wenn der Boden der Tradition wegbricht. Das Motiv der Blume, das in diesem Bild dominiert, findet sich sehr häufig in Birkhäusers Bildern. Augen werden als Blumen gemalt oder Figuren werden in blumige Gewänder gesteckt – in solchen floralen Gestaltungen scheint sich das Wunder der mathematischen Form auszudrücken; es wird sichtbar im Werden des lebendigen Wesens. Blumen repräsentieren, schreibt Jung an einer Stelle seiner *Erinnerungen*, die unschuldigen Gedanken des Schöpfers: «Mit dem Pflanzenreich begann die irdische Entwicklung der Gotteswelt als eine Art unmittelbare Mitteilung. Es war, als ob man dem Schöpfer, der sich unbeobachtet wähnte, über die Schulter geschaut hätte, wie er Spielzeug oder Dekorationsstücke anfertigte. Demgegenüber waren der Mensch und die […] Tiere selbständig gewordene Gottesteile. Darum konnten sie aus freien Stücken herumgehen und ihre Wohnorte wählen. Die Pflanzenwelt dagegen war auf Gedeih und Verderb an ihren Standort gebunden. Sie drückte nicht nur die Schönheit, sondern auch die Gedanken der Gotteswelt aus, ohne irgendwelche Absicht oder Abweichung.»[7] In unserem Bild sind diese wundersamen Gebilde des schöpferischen Geistes dargestellt, unter denen auch der Mensch erscheint. Obwohl er leider unendlich viel komplizierter und problematischer ist als eine Pflanze, scheint der feurige Geburtsprozess auf den Menschen zuzulaufen. Im Sinne Meister Eckharts wäre der Mensch das Ziel: «Eines jeden Kornes Natur zielt auf Weizen, und alles Metalls Natur zielt auf Gold, und jedes Gebären zielt auf den Menschen.»[8] Ziel der Evolution ist, zumindest auf dieser Erde, das menschliche Bewusstsein; wir wissen nicht, was die göttlichen Kräfte durch uns noch schaffen werden.

Als nächstes malte Birkhäuser einen schönen, dunkelhäutigen Jüngling mit vier Armen, der auf einem zottligen, weissen Pferd reitet, das einem Eber ähnlich ist («Puer aeternus», Abb. 11). Aus der ausgestreckten Hand des Jünglings wächst eine magische Blume heraus. Jung, der die drei Bilder «Tier im Berg», «Feuergeburt» und «Puer aeternus» im Original betrachten konnte, kommentierte: «Das Tier, das im Berg gefangen ist, stellt einen unbewussten Inhalt dar, der einen starken Druck ausübt. Es ist etwas in der Seele, vielleicht auch im Körper, das eine Explosion hervorrufen könnte. Oft kennzeichnen unangemessene Gefühlsausbrüche eine solche Situation.» Über die «Feuergeburt» äusserte er: «Jetzt bricht der Inhalt aus den heissen Wellen der Libido [am rechten Bildrand] hervor, man könnte auch sagen: aus den Wogen der Emotion, des aufgewühlten Gefühls. Solche wellenartige Linien erscheinen oft in Bildern von Gefühlstypen. Es ist schöpferische Energie – diese Formen erinnern an Ektoplasma. Das ist es, was Goethe mit ‹Die Schöpfung! Urbild alles Lebendigen!› [im *Faust*] im Sinn hatte. Der Mann mit dem satyrhaften Kopf hat etwas Dämonisches an sich, er ist der Anfang eines teuflischen Schreckens.» Jung fuhr fort: «Die Schöpfung ist ganz und gar dämonisch, wunderbar – ein ehrfurchtgebietendes und furchterregendes Geheimnis. Wenn man bedenkt, wie die Raupe ihren Kokon spinnt und wie die Puppe schon die Gestalt des künftigen Schmetterlings annimmt, während die Raupe sich noch in milchige Flüssigkeit auflöst [...]. Wir nehmen immer an, dass wir dafür verantwortlich sind, die Stiele an den Kirschen anzubringen – in Wirklichkeit sind wir aber nur das Werkzeug der Natur!» In Bezug auf das dritte Bild, den schwarzen Jüngling auf dem weissen Pferd, den «Puer aeternus», urteilte er: «Das dunkle Tier ist befreit,

7 C. G. Jung: *Erinnerungen, Träume, Gedanken*. Hrsg. von Aniela Jaffé, Zürich, Stuttgart: Rascher, 1967, S. 72 f.

8 Meister Eckhart, Predigt 38, in: *Meister Eckhart. Werke I*. Texte und Übersetzungen von Josef Quint, hrsg. v. Niklaus Largier. Frankfurt a. M.: Deutscher Klassiker Verlag, 1993, S. 407.

und nun reitet es in Gestalt des weissen, eberartigen Pferdes durch die weiten Himmel. Es stellt den weissen Pegasus dar, der den Wassermann bringt, oder den *puer aeternus, albus et ater*. Der Gott offenbart sich jedermann. Das ist, was die Leute nicht verstehen können! Ich kann hier gar nicht alles erzählen, was zu diesem Bild des Puer gehörte: Es hat mit der fortschreitenden Menschwerdung Gottes zu tun.»

Als Peter Birkhäuser begann, sich dem kollektiven Unbewussten zuzuwenden und diesem erlaubte, durch ihn hindurch Ausdruck zu finden, tauchten in seinen Bildern viele sehr dunkle und unheimliche Motive auf: ein Mann mit gespaltenem Antlitz (Abb. 2), ein buckliger Junge, der aus der Kanalisation nach oben steigt und eine Grubenlampe trägt (Abb. 5), ein grüner Weltraumdämon mit Pferdegesicht, der sich eines einsamen Flugzeugs bemächtigt, ein vieräugiges Gesicht, das einen verängstigten, sich verzweifelt abwendenden Mann mit Blitzen beschiesst, und viele andere. Es ist ein Pandämonium von seltsamen und furchterregenden Erscheinungen, das an Hieronymus Bosch denken lässt. Wenn das Unbewusste endlich ins Bewusstsein kommen darf, trägt es oft erschreckende und dunkle Züge. In dieser Zeit des Übergangs, als innere Bilder in die Welt der äusseren Realität einbrachen, malte Birkhäuser unter anderem auch eine alte, hexenhafte Frau mit dem Gesicht einer Katze, ein Porträt, das Dr. Jung in seinem Besitz hatte und in seinem Arbeitszimmer aufbewahrte (Abb. 3).

Peter Birkhäuser, der als Empfindungstyp eine hohe Sensibilität für die schöne Form besitzt, litt sehr unter der Anforderung, dem Dunklen und Abgründigen Gestalt zu geben. Im Gegensatz zu anderen modernen Malern, die die Zerstörung der äusseren Wirklichkeit dadurch wiederzugeben suchten, dass sie ihre Gegenstände zertrümmerten, verzerrten und generell abstossend wiedergaben, hat Birkhäuser die Form an sich nicht verworfen. Er wollte selbst die dunkelsten, unheimlichsten und destruktivsten Kräfte in sorgfältig gestalteten Formen und Figuren festhalten. Das verleiht seinen Bildern ihren einzigartigen Charakter. Viele moderne Künstler, die sich der inneren Phantasiewelt zuwenden, versuchen den Unterschied zur äusseren Realität durch eine gewisse Unschärfe anzudeuten oder indem sie Motive ineinander blenden, als wären mehrere Fotografien übereinander aufgenommen worden (z. B. Chagall). Birkhäuser wählte einen anderen Weg, er versah seine Figuren mit feinstofflichen Eigenschaften oder gab ihnen eine geisterhafte Transparenz. Dies ebenso wie die dunklen Farben, die er häufig für den Hintergrund verwendet, verleiht seinen Bildern eine «nächtliche» Qualität, die die Realität des Unbewussten vermittelt. Ein Analysand von mir, ein Empfindungstyp, der nie ganz an die Wirklichkeit des

Unbewussten glauben konnte, war überwältigt von diesen Gemälden und rief aus: «Jetzt sehe ich zum ersten Mal die Kräfte, die ich fürchtete und von denen ich immer gehofft hatte, sie mögen nicht existieren. Jetzt endlich sind sie real für mich.»

Der überwältigend bedrohliche und gefährliche Aspekt des Unbewussten ist in vielen frühen Arbeiten Birkhäusers vertreten; jene abgründige Dunkelheit findet sich auch in einem Gemälde, das er «Der Ausgestossene» (Abb. 10) nennt. Es zeigt eine Art Dämon, der über eine Industriestadt hinwegschreitet und sich von ihr entfernt. Wieder erscheint die Stadt in farblosen, grauen Tönen – die unnatürliche, tote, «technische», rationale Welt bezeichnend, aus der die schöpferischen Kräfte der Phantasie wie auch der Geist der Natur vertrieben sind. Mitten durch das Gesicht des «Ausgestossenen» verläuft eine Schattenlinie, die sein Antlitz in zwei Hälften teilt. Es handelt sich wahrscheinlich um den *Mercurius duplex* der Alchemisten, den göttlichen Geist in der Materie, der «gut mit den Guten und böse mit den Bösen» ist. Wir selbst sind gespalten und deshalb kann sich auch der göttliche Geist der Materie nicht in seiner Ganzheit ausdrücken – er nimmt einen Doppelcharakter an. Man könnte sagen: «Das Gequälte quält und das Gespaltene spaltet!»

Die Füsse des Dämons sind steif, plump und unnatürlich; man spürt, dass er Dinge ungewollt niedertrampeln könnte, wie auch das «Tier im Berg» (Abb. 8) unfreiwillig zerstörerisch agieren könnte. Ein anderes Bild zeigt einen zornigen Zwerg mit bleiernen Füssen. Blei ist traditionell das dem Saturn zugeordnete Metall, ein Symbol für die «niederdrückende» Qualität des Unbewussten, jene Depression, die zugleich die *prima materia* aller Schöpferkraft ist. Die bleiernen Füsse verleihen dem «Ausgestossenen» den Doppelaspekt des Verderbers und Erlösers. Die Regenbogenfarben des Flammenschweifs, den er mit sich zieht, deuten ebenfalls auf einen rettenden Aspekt hin. Im alchemistischen Prozess führt das Erhitzen des Bleis unmittelbar nach der *nigredo* in ein Stadium, in dem «alle Farben erscheinen». Die alten Meister sagen, dass dies der Moment ist, in dem die Seele (der Materie) erscheint.[9] Die Seele ist ein Geist (im Sinne von Dampf), und das ist wahrscheinlich der Grund, warum der feurige Kometenschweif in unserem Bild wie Ektoplasma aussieht: Es ist sozusagen Seelenmaterial. Der «Ausgestossene» hat also viel mit Mercurius, dem «Geist in der Materie» der Alchemisten, gemeinsam, der von unserem materialistisch orientierten Zeitalter verbannt wurde und alles Leben und alle Farben

9 Vgl. C. G. Jung, *Mysterium Coniunctionis*, GW 14/2, § 51 f.

mitgenommen hat. Es gibt noch eine weitere grosse Gefahr, die in diesem Bild dargestellt ist: Mercurius wendet sich nach links (wie der Behemoth in Abb. 8) und bewegt sich somit auf das Unbewusste zu, als ob er im Begriff wäre, darin zu verschwinden. Den Schweif, den er hinter sich herzieht, gemahnt so gesehen an die Möglichkeit, die Stadt hinter ihm in Brand zu stecken.

Insofern wir alle in der Gefahr schweben, durch Feuer und Radioaktivität getötet zu werden, insbesondere in den grossen Industriestädten, vermittelt dieser feurige Schweif etwas sehr Unmittelbares und Erschreckendes: Wird der göttliche Geist in der Natur und in unserem Unbewussten, diese durch unseren Rationalismus und unsere ausbeuterische Einstellung vergewaltigte, geschändete göttliche Macht, uns töten, bevor sie uns verlässt? Wird sie unsere ganze Welt niedertrampeln und ins Unbekannte zurück verschwinden, aus dem sie gekommen ist? Es gibt aber auch hoffnungsvolle und versöhnliche Elemente in diesem Werk: Der Dämon hat weisses Haar wie Gottvater – er ist von uralter, grosser Weisheit. Der vielfarbige, feurige Schweif lässt zudem an den Regenbogen denken, den Gott schuf, um sich an sein Versprechen zu erinnern, die Menschheit nie wieder ausrotten zu wollen, wie er es mit der Sintflut versucht hatte. Dieser dämonische Gott trägt also immer doch das uralte Erinnerungszeichen und grosse Symbol der Versöhnung mit sich. Es hängt wie ein ständiges Damoklesschwert und Schutzschild zugleich über unseren Köpfen.

Das Gesicht des «Ausgestossenen» ist von einer blauen und bläulich-grünen Farbe, worin angedeutet ist, dass er aus den Tiefen des Wassers und aus der Welt der Vegetation stammt, zwei Naturbereiche, die wir zu unserem eigenen Schaden mehr denn je unentwegt verschmutzen und zerstören. Die zu Krallen geformten Hände und das rötliche Fellkleid weisen auf die animalische Natur dieses Dämons hin. Vor dem Hintergrund seiner Mercurius-Natur sind diese Eigenschaften so zu verstehen, dass sich in ihm das Mineral-, Pflanzen- und Tierreich vereinen. Die Krallen und das Fell sind nicht die einzigen auffälligen Merkmale – der «Ausgestossene» ist auch wie erwähnt durch ein gespaltenes Antlitz und einen Buckel gekennzeichnet. Bekanntlich werden missgebildete Menschen häufig als Glücksbringer betrachtet. In Italien kann man zum Beispiel beobachten, dass sich Menschen um einen Buckligen scharen, weil es Glück bringt, seinen Buckel zu berühren. In unserem Bild dagegen erscheint der Bucklige entstellt – er ist als Krüppel gezeichnet. In seiner Gespaltenheit und Schattenhaftigkeit erinnert er wie gesagt an den gespaltenen Mann, den Birkhäuser vor dem «Ausgestossenen» malte (Abb. 2).

Das Motiv des Buckligen erscheint in einem anderen frühen Werk in Gestalt eines blassen rothaarigen Knaben, der eine Leiter aus dem Abwasserkanal hinaufsteigt (Abb. 5). Diese Figur repräsentiert den Outcast in menschlicher Gestalt: als entstellter, unglücklicher, kranker Knabe der Unterschicht, der Mitleid und Ehrfurcht zugleich erweckt. Dr. Jung äusserte einmal in einem Interview mit einem Stadtplaner, der moderne Mensch habe ein Stück eigenes Land ganz besonders nötig – ein kleines Haus oder einen Garten, wo er seine Vorstellungen und seine schöpferischen Phantasien ausleben kann (was auch der Grund für den grossen Erfolg der Kleingartenbewegung ist).[10] Wenn man Menschen in Plattenbausiedlungen, kollektiven «Zementkästen», zusammenpfercht, können sie einem elementaren Lebensbedürfnis nicht nachkommen; oft wird die Gesellschaft oder die Wirtschaftsordnung für diesen Zustand verantwortlich gemacht. Wenn die elementaren Instinkte des Menschen nicht mehr mitleben können, wird er destruktiv.

Im rechten Auge des «Ausgestossenen» erblickt man (v.a. wenn das andere Auge verdeckt wird) einen Anflug von mörderischem Wahnsinn, während das linke Auge voller Leid nach oben gerichtet ist, als ob von dort Hilfe zu bekommen wäre. Dieser gegensätzliche Blick scheint Ausdruck des Zustands des Teils der Psyche zu sein, den das Kollektiv aus dem modernen Leben *ausgestossen* hat: Es ist noch nicht entschieden, ob der «Ausgestossene» sich in schiere Zerstörungswut verwandeln oder ob sein Leiden eine hilfreiche Veränderung unserer kollektiven Einstellung bewirken wird. Es ist die Dualität und Spannung dieser Situation, die sich im Gemälde des «Ausgestossenen» spiegelt.

Der «Zwillingsfisch» (Abb. 12) ist ein späteres Werk; auffällig ist die Steigerung der Farbintensität und des Lichts. Es ist, als bräche die schillernde Oberfläche des Wassers auf und ein Auge (vielleicht das Spiegelbild des Auges des Betrachters) blickte aus der blauen Tiefe herauf. Es ist das Auge, das uns aus den Tiefen unserer eigenen Seele anschaut und uns das eigenartige Gefühl vermittelt, dass wir bei allem, was wir tun, von einer überpersönlichen Macht gesehen werden. Die Erfahrung, von einem Grösseren gesehen zu werden, beschrieb Paulus im Brief an die Korinther: «Jetzt erkenne ich stückweise; dann aber werde ich erkennen, wie ich erkannt bin.» (1 Kor 13,12) Wenn wir objektive Erkenntnis über uns selbst erlangen wollen, Erkenntnis, die nicht aus subjektiven Gedanken hervor-

10 Mitte des 19. Jahrhunderts entwickelte sich parallel zur Turnbewegung die Idee, kleine Flecken in den Brachflächen rund um die Städte an Menschen zu vermieten, die über kein eigenes Land verfügen, um sie als Gärten zu nutzen.

geht, müssen wir versuchen herauszufinden, wie dieses andere Auge in der Tiefe unserer Seele uns sieht, denn in diesem Sinne sind wir erkannt, bevor wir erkennen werden.

In der Alchemie wird die Symbolik der Fischaugen oftmals mit der Symbolik der Lichtfunken in eins gesetzt,[11] weshalb Gerhard Dorns Erläuterung über das Phänomen des Funkens auf das berühmte alchemistische Fischaugen-Motiv bezogen werden kann: «So wird er [der Adept] mit seinen geistigen Augen wahrnehmen, wie einige Funken mehr und mehr [und] von Tag zu Tag durchschimmern und zu einem so grossen Licht anwachsen, dass in der Folgezeit alles bekannt wird, was ihm notwendig ist.» Jung kommentiert: «Dieses Licht ist das *lumen naturae*, welches das Bewusstsein erleuchtet, und die *scintillae* [Funken] sind keimhafte Luminositäten, die aus dem Dunkel des Unbewussten hervorleuchten.»[12]

In unserem Gemälde markiert das blaue Auge des Wassers den Gegensatz zum roten Auge des Fisches, das zugleich die Mitte einer Blume bildet. Dieses rote Fischauge ähnelt in gewisser Hinsicht dem Auge des «Tiers im Berg». Beide sind von der Gestalt eines Mandalas, wobei das Zentrum, das zunächst nur in der gleichmässig geordneten Form zum Ausdruck kommt, zu «sehen» beginnt, was im Wasser ist – und zwar mit grosser Leidenschaft (daher die rote Farbe). Dieses Auge könnte für die neue Sicht stehen, die durch die vierte Funktion ins Bewusstsein gelangt; sein Erwachen ermöglicht Einblick in bisher unbekannte Bereiche des Lebens. In Birkhäusers Typologie wäre es das Auge der Intuition, das ihn befähigt, die bedeutenden Mächte des kollektiven Unbewussten zu sehen.

Der Fisch ist semi-transparent, was ihm eine spirituelle Qualität verleiht.[13] Im Inneren seines Körpers sind zwei schöne Jünglinge vereint, die sich umarmen. Wer sind diese jungen Männer, die die durchsichtige Qualität des subtilen Körpers und die zauberhafte Schönheit des Fisches miteinander teilen? Der Fisch als Symbol erscheint in Verbindung mit anderen Motiven in vielen bekannten Mythen. Nicht nur Christus wurde traditionell als Fisch dargestellt – es gibt, wie Dr. Jung in *Aion* darlegt, viele Beispiele von Fischern und Fischen, die aus den Tiefen des Unbewussten kommen, um die Menschheit zu retten.

---

11 S. dazu: C. G. Jung: «Theoretische Überlegungen zum Wesen des Psychischen» in: *Die Dynamik des Unbewussten*, GW 8, § 394.

12 Zit. nach: C. G. Jung: «Theoretische Überlegungen zum Wesen des Psychischen» in: *Die Dynamik des Unbewussten,* GW 8, § 389.

13 *Diaphanitas* oder Durchsichtigkeit wurde von den Alchemisten als Hinweis auf eine spirituelle Natur verstanden.

Auch von dem grossen babylonischen Weisheitslehrer Oannes wurde angenommen, dass er in Gestalt eines Fischs aus dem Meer aufgestiegen war, entsprechend trugen seine Priester Gewänder aus Fischhaut. Die hinduistische Gottheit Vishnu tauchte in Gestalt eines Fischs in die Fluten hinab, um die heiligen Schriften der Veden vor ihrer Vernichtung zu retten. Dass Birkhäusers «Zwillingsfisch» eine Erlösergestalt in Form des schönen Jünglings in sich trägt, ist somit nicht weiter verwunderlich. Derselbe Jüngling erscheint im bereits erwähnten «Puer aeternus»-Gemälde auf einem wilden, weissen Eber-Pferd reitend, eine magische aus seiner Hand hervorwachsende Blume haltend (Abb. 11).

Der *puer aeternus*, der aus dem Unbewussten kommt, bringt die «heilige Quelle» in die Welt, von der Vergil schon träumte. Vom menschlichen Standpunkt aus gesehen, könnte dieser neue, rettende Inhalt die Möglichkeit einer neuen religiösen Erfahrung als eines inneren Geschehens darstellen. Das Motiv der zwei Jünglinge im Fisch lässt mich an einen berühmten Vers aus den *Upanishaden* denken: « Zwei schön beflügelte, verbundene Freunde / Umarmen einen und denselben Baum; / Einer von ihnen speist die süsse Beere, / Der andre schaut, nicht essend, nur herab.»[14] Die «Zwillingsfreunde» repräsentieren elementare Gegensätze in unserer Psyche, zugleich stehen sie für gegensätzliche psychische Einstellungen: Extraversion («essen» wurde in Indien als die Welt verspeisen verstanden) und Introversion.

In unserem westlichen Teil der Welt stehen die Gegensätze in einer viel stärkeren Spannung zueinander als im Kulturraum Asiens, nicht selten liegen sie sogar im Streit miteinander. Horus und Seth in Ägypten ebenso wie Christus und Satan im Abendland sind zu feindlichen Brüdern geworden, zu sich gegenseitig bekämpfenden Prinzipien von Gut und Böse. Der lichte Bruder Christus lehnte seinen Schatten ab, der dadurch zu seinem Gegner und sogar Feind wurde. Diese Spaltung hat nun unsere gesamte Zivilisation erfasst, in der die Gegensätze sich bekriegen und in wachsender Verbitterung erstarrt sind. Gleichwohl sind die gegensätzlichen Hälften Brüder, die aus denselben Tiefen der unbewussten Psyche stammen. Eine apokryphe Schrift der Bogomilen, einer mittelalterlichen christlichen Religionsgemeinschaft, schildert die Gegensätze interessanterweise als Fische, die wie zusammengespannte Ochsen die Oberfläche des Wassers durchpflügen. Jung schreibt über diese Konstellation: «Der Vergleich der beiden Fische mit einem Joch Ochsen, die vor den Pflug gespannt sind, verdient besondere Aufmerksamkeit: Die Ochsen stellen die

14 Shvetâshvatara-Upanishad, IV,6; zit. nach: C. G. Jung, *Symbole der Wandlung*, GW 5, § 296, Anm. 61.

treibende Kraft des Pfluges dar. In gleicher Weise bedeuten daher die Fische die treibenden Kräfte der kommenden Welt, das heisst des zukünftigen Bewusstseinszustandes. [...] Das Pflügen, das heisst die Inbesitznahme der Erde, geschieht *patris praecepto*, auf Befehl des Vaters. Gott hat also die Enantiodromie, die im Jahre 1000 begann, nicht nur vorausgesehen, sondern auch beabsichtigt. Der Weltmonat der Fische soll von zwei Prinzipien regiert sein. Die Fische sind hier, wie die Ochsen, parallel, das heisst auf das gleiche Ziel ausgerichtet, obschon der eine Christus, der andere aber der Antichristus ist.»[15]

Das Prinzip der inneren Dualität stellt sich in unserem Bild, das nur einen Fisch aufweist, in den beiden Jünglingen dar. Die Gegensätze erscheinen nicht nur erneuert, sondern darüber hinaus in liebevoller Umarmung vereint. Der Fisch trägt sie nach unten in die Tiefe des Wassers und nach links. Wahrscheinlich können sie sich nur deshalb vereinigen. Tauchte der Fisch noch weiter und tiefer ins Wasser hinunter, könnten sich die beiden Jünglinge vielleicht sogar auflösen und wieder zu einer göttlichen Gestalt werden. Wenn ihre Vereinigung vollzogen ist, kann der Fisch nach oben zurückkehren und ein neues rettendes Symbol gebären: die Gestalt eines Erlösers oder die Doppelgestalt vereinter Zwillingsbrüder in völliger Harmonie, wie die Ashvins in Indien oder Castor und Pollux, die grossen Helfer in Seenot.[16] Wie Jung in *Aion* hervorhebt, hat das Symbol des Fischs häufig einen doppelten beziehungsweise hermaphroditischen Aspekt, denn es handelt sich um eine *complexio oppositorum*; entsprechend wird der Fisch im biblischen Kontext auch als «wunderbare Speise» gesehen – «er ist die eucharistische Speise der Vollendeten (*teleioi*)».[17]

Der «Zwillingsfisch» ist nicht Birkhäusers letztes Bild. Er arbeitet weiter und ich bin immer wieder überrascht, welche neuen Wendungen seine Motive und sein Stil nehmen. Er bleibt nicht stehen – der kreative Dämon treibt ihn wie so viele Künstler an, immer wieder neue Wege auszuprobieren. Der Schaffensdrang in ihm ist so stark, dass er seine ganze Kraft aufsparen muss, um ihm gerecht zu werden. Und so lebt Peter Birkhäuser ein eher introvertiertes und zurückgezogenes Leben mit seiner Familie in Binningen bei Basel. Für effektvolle Inszenierungen á la Salvador Dalí hat er keine Zeit, und doch erreichen seine Bilder die Menschen. Als einmal eines seiner Gemälde in einer Druckerei reproduziert

15 C. G. Jung, *Aion,* GW 9/II, § 231.
16 Vgl. C. G. Jung, *Symbole der Wandlung*, GW 5, § 296.
17 C. G. Jung, *Aion,* GW 9/II, § 237. Die *teleioi* waren die Vollkommenen, diejenigen, die Vollkommenheit in einem spezifisch gnostischen Sinn der erleuchteten Gotteserkenntnis erreicht hatten.

wurde, rief eine junge Mitarbeiterin bei Birkhäuser an – sie hatte den Abzug gesehen und war so beeindruckt, dass sie die Bilder dieses Malers kennenlernen wollte. Sie kam schliesslich mit einer Gruppe von Freunden ins Atelier. Die jungen Besucher waren begeistert und brachten den Bildern viel Verständnis entgegen. Dieses Beispiel zeigt vielleicht, dass sich die jüngere Generation auf ganz natürliche Weise den inneren Tatsachen der Psyche annähert, die Jung als einsamer Pionier weit vor seiner Zeit entdeckt hatte. Die einzige Enttäuschung der jungen Leute bestand darin, dass der Maler nichts mit dem bärtigen Bohemien gemein hatte, den sie sich vorgestellt hatten. Jeder, der Peter Birkhäuser kennt, kann das verborgene Feuer in seinem Inneren spüren, das er mit seiner ruhigen und introvertierten Art überdeckt. Ein junger Mann, der ihn einmal in seiner Werkstatt besucht hatte, fasste seinen Eindruck so zusammen: «Als ich das kleine Gartenatelier verliess, blickte ich voller Verwunderung zurück und wollte nicht glauben, dass diese kleine Hütte eine Heimstatt so kostbarer und überwältigender Mächte war.»

Aus dem Englischen übersetzt von Michaela Kopp-Marx, 2023

38
PORTRAIT OF C. G. JUNG

An example of Peter Birkhäuser's style in the earlier phase of his art. This drawing was a commission for a birthday present for Jung. Crayon, April 1958

38
PORTRÄT VON C. G. JUNG

Ein Beispiel für die Kunst, wie Birkhäuser sie in seiner früheren Schaffenszeit gepflegt hat. Die Zeichnung war eine Auftragsarbeit. Sie diente als Geburtstagsgeschenk für C. G. Jung. Kreide, April 1958

LIST OF PLATES

BILDERVERZEICHNIS

Index

Register

Eva Wertenschlag-Birkhäuser & Kaspar Birkhäuser

Der rote Faden

Malerei und Grafik von Peter Birkhäuser

Bildband mit zahlreichen Erstveröffentlichungen, gebunden

Der Künstler Peter Birkhäuser (1911–1976) war ein bekannter Basler Grafiker und Plakatgestalter. Weniger bekannt war bislang sein Wirken als Maler. Seine Malerei umfasst ein überraschendes Werk, in dem nicht nur seine innere, seelische und geistige Welt zum Ausdruck gebracht wird, sondern auch eine beeindruckende Dimension kollektiv bedeutsamer Inhalte, die ins Bewusstsein drängen.

Dieser Aspekt seiner Kunst sprengt den biographischen und lokalen Rahmen und macht sein Werk zu einer gültigen Zeitaussage.

Der rote Faden enthält neben Ausschnitten aus dem grafischen Oeuvre über hundert Abbildungen von Gemälden des Künstlers; mehr als 50 davon werden hier erstmals veröffentlicht.

248 Seiten, ISBN 978-3-85630-751-6

Eva Wertenschlag-Birkhäuser

Windows on Eternity: The Paintings of Peter Birkhäuser

With an Essay by Marie-Louise von Franz

Many of the dream images painted by Swiss artist Peter Birkhäuser (1911-76) portray the big problems of our time, as experienced one individual: our divisiveness, possession by unconscious factors, suffering from the loss of religious values, the "unknown God" knocking at the door and wanting to enter, our inability to understand evil, the world of the feminine yearning for redemption, and so on.

Because the paintings of Birkhäuser come from the deep wells of dreams and give them authentic form, they are mirrors of healing processes in the soul. Marie-Louise von Franz said of Birkhäuser's work: "His paintings are not depictions of his own problems, but rather seek to reveal what is taking place in the depths of the collective unconscious in all of the people of our time. Because of this, they are not easy to decipher: they are simply there, and wish to be experienced".

This book is an attempt to track down the meanings of the mysteries in the work of Peter Birkhäuser. Included are 53 reproductions of paintings by the artist.

200 pages, 53 color plates, ISBN 978-3-85630-715-8

ENGLISH TITLES FROM DAIMON

Ruth Ammann - *The Enchantment of Gardens*
Susan R. Bach - *Life Paints its Own Span*
Diana Baynes Jansen - *Jung's Apprentice: A Biography of Helton Godwin Baynes*
John Beebe (Ed.) - *Terror, Violence and the Impulse to Destroy*
E.A. Bennet - *Meetings with Jung*
Sibylle Birkhäuser-Oeri - *Mother Figures in Fairy Tales*
W.H. Bleek / L.C. Lloyd (Ed.) - *Specimens of Bushman Folklore*
Tess Castleman - *Threads, Knots, Tapestries*
- *Sacred Dream Circles*
Renate Daniel - *Taking the Fear out of the Night*
- *The Self: Quest for Meaning in a Changing World*
- *Psyche and Soma*
Eranos Yearbook 69 - *Eranos Reborn*
Eranos Yearbook 70 - *Love on a Fragile Thread*
Eranos Yearbook 71 - *Beyond Masters*
Eranos Yearbook 72 - *Soul between Enchantment and Disenchantment*
Eranos Yearbook 73 - *The World and its Shadow*
Eranos Yearbook 74 - *The Age of Immediacy at the Test of Meaning*
Eranos Yearbook 75 - *Life, Individual, Community, and the Thought of the Absolute ...*
Michael Escamilla - *Bleuler, Jung, and the Schizophrenias*
Heinrich Karl Fierz - *Jungian Psychiatry*
John Fraim - *Battle of Symbols*
Liliane Frey-Rohn - *Friedrich Nietzsche, A Psychological Approach*
Marion Gallbach - *Learning from Dreams*
Ralph Goldstein (Ed.) - *Images, Meanings & Connections: Essays in Memory of Susan Bach*
Yael Haft - *Hands: Archetypal Chirology*
Fred Gustafson - *The Black Madonna of Einsiedeln*
Daniel Hell - *Soul-Hunger: The Feeling Human Being and the Life-Sciences*
Siegmund Hurwitz - *Lilith, the first Eve*
Aniela Jaffé - *Reflections on the Life and Dreams of C.G. Jung With a Historical Commentary by Elena Fischli*
- *The Myth of Meaning*
- *Was C.G. Jung a Mystic?*
- *From the Life and Work of C.G. Jung*
- *Death Dreams and Ghosts*
C.G. Jung - *The Solar Myths and Opicinus de Canistris*
Verena Kast - *A Time to Mourn*
- *Sisyphus*
Hayao Kawai - *Dreams, Myths and Fairy Tales in Japan*
James Kirsch - *The Reluctant Prophet*
Eva Langley-Dános - *Prison on Wheels: Ravensbrück to Burgau*
Rivkah Schärf Kluger - *The Gilgamesh Epic*
Yehezkel Kluger & Nomi Kluger-Nash - *RUTH in the Light of Mythology, Legend and Kabbalah*
Paul Kugler (Ed.) - *Jungian Perspectives on Clinical Supervision*
Paul Kugler - *The Alchemy of Discourse*
Rafael López-Pedraza - *Cultural Anxiety*
- *Hermes and his Children*
Alan McGlashan - *The Savage and Beautiful Country*
- *Gravity & Levity*
Gregory McNamee (Ed.) - *The Girl Who Made Stars: Bushman Folklore*
- *The North Wind and the Sun & Other Fables of Aesop*
Gitta Mallasz / Hanna Dallos - *Talking with Angels*